TEXTUAL HEALING

How a Cellphone Saved a
Single, Sinking, Suburban Mom

TEXTUAL HEALING

How a Cellphone Saved a
Single, Sinking, Suburban Mom

Annie North

Textual Healing: How a Cellphone Saved a Single, Sinking, Suburban Mom

Copyright © 2018 by Annie North

This edition published by Highpoint Life.
For information, write to info@highpointpubs.com.

FIRST EDITION

ISBN: 978-0-9989840-5-6

North, Annie
Textual Healing: How a Cellphone Saved a Single, Sinking, Suburban Mom

Summary: "*Textual Healing: How a Cellphone Saved a Single, Sinking, Suburban Mom* is the story of how Annie North learned about love, adventure, possibility, and opportunity through strangers on cellphones. By inventing new characters within herself, she became a powerful muse for her men and in return, their love for her was the strength she needed to become the woman who had been waiting to be set free." – Provided by publisher.

ISBN: 978-0-9989840-5-6

Library of Congress Control Number: 2018950285

DESIGN BY SARAH CLAREHART

10 9 8 7 6 5 4 3 2 1

Contents

I've always had a hard time reconciling the old adage, "Don't talk to strangers," with the suggestion that "A stranger is just a friend you haven't met yet." I can remember being in the grocery store with my son, who was in preschool at the time, and as people tend to do to pass time in the checkout line, the woman behind me began to ask him questions to keep him occupied while I emptied my cart.

My son very sternly told her, "My teacher told me not to talk to strangers. Please go away."

The woman stood there, looking at my son with a sort of awe that he had learned the lesson so thoroughly, while at the same time looking as though she'd just been punched in the stomach for trying to be nice.

I spent an awkward few minutes trying to put together a decent explanation for my son about it being acceptable if a parent is around.

"But you don't know her either, Mommy," was his quick rebuttal, and I couldn't argue with him, at least not in the time it took to get the Cheerios and apple juice bagged. I gave the woman a pathetic smile, gathered my son, and left the store. But I spent the rest of the day, and plenty of time thereafter, pondering that little dilemma.

I like strangers. Even as a little kid myself, after hearing the horror stories of other girls who were whisked away in nondescript vans after making that fateful choice, I thought I was kind of a badass for tempting fate every time I dared utter words to people to whom I hadn't been formally introduced.

What was a stranger, anyway? I mean, what if I was over at my friend's house, and her brother's friend's mom came to pick him up? They're strangers to me, but if my best friend can vouch for them, isn't it all just semantics? Doesn't someone know everyone? Long before Six Degrees of Kevin Bacon, I was trying to justify that we are all connected in some way, and it's up to each of us to recognize that if we want our world to get both bigger and more intimate.

My dad used to say that he loved Ireland for the singular reason that you could drive around all day, looking at sheep and the emerald-green countryside, and when you got so tired you couldn't keep going, you could knock on anyone's door and they'd take you in for the night and even feed you. This had been his experience during his two or three visits there, and he wrote down the name of every single person he encountered, and kept in touch until the day he died.

My dad loved that happenstance kind of connection, and I always wanted to experience that same level of intimacy with strangers. I wanted to have a notebook like his, filled with names of people I didn't know but for a few moments, with whom I'd keep in touch and forever call them friends. It was such a romantic notion.

My first such encounter came as a young adult traveling alone for the first time, while waiting on a train platform for the Amtrak. I saw an older gentleman sitting on a bench alone, and I asked him if I was on the right track.

"Stick with me," he replied, and as the train approached, I helped him with his cane and briefcase, and we settled in for the long ride.

Shortly after we'd made our introductions and a little more small talk, he declared that he was going to the bar car.

"I didn't mean to keep you," I said sadly, "I guess this is where we say goodbye."

"Nonsense," he replied tersely. "I've been up since 5 a.m. and I need some coffee. I'll be happy to get you some, if you'll keep an eye on my briefcase for me."

I agreed, and he disappeared for close to half an hour, and two stops. I was beginning to worry that he'd ditched me, when he returned and jovially exclaimed, "Ah! You're still here! Thought you'd have taken off by now."

"Why would I do that?" I asked.

"Because you're holding my briefcase with $32,000 cash in it," he said, matter-of-factly. "I thought you'd have rifled through and made off with it by now."

I was hooked. Instantly fascinated that a seventy-year old man would leave a girl on a train with a briefcase full of cash, I suddenly felt like Ingrid Bergman or Kim Novak from those old movies my dad and I used to watch. It didn't even matter why he had it; I spent the rest of the trip asking one question after another, trying to learn as much about my new friend as I could before we parted, my curiosity ignited forever. I never forgot that sense of wonder of entering someone else's world, the excitement of what brought us together at that juncture, and how that meeting might affect me thereafter.

So now you know I like to talk to strangers. But the other thing to know about me is that I sometimes take it too far into the other direction, what some might call *stranger danger*, because I am so comfortable being intimate with a new face in the crowd. My curiosity came to me courtesy of my surrounding family, whose relationships—and the lines that separate or join them—were never properly defined.

As the youngest girl in a very large family, I had oodles of people around me all the time during my formative years. Friends, neighbors, and relatives alike would converge on our house, my home, and simply blend in until it was time to leave. Most of the kids I knew had a few siblings within a few years' range, with common reference points: the same math teacher, or the aunt who always smears her lipstick when she kisses hello, or the grandparents in Florida. I had six older brothers, from two to fourteen years older than me, all in different stages of their own lives. They ran the gamut from wildly popular to anti-social, from athletic to bookworm, from happy to miserable. One thing they all had in common though, was a baby sister whom they loved, and protected with an easy vengeance, regardless of whether it was on the playground at recess, or visiting them at their college dorm, sometimes both in the same day. As the offspring of my devoutly Catholic father, who made most of his sacrifices in the name of setting a good example, these guys were my heroes, and I remember praying each night that I would be worthy of them. Because of that love and protection, there was not much dating for me, the natural result of the double-edged sword that on one side had no guy being good enough for their little sister; and on the other side having said sister falling for such a guy and disappointing them. Because I never considered myself dating material, I learned how to relate to all sorts of boys without fear. All those brothers and all their friends of all ages and backgrounds acquainted me with a nice microcosm of how guys think, act, and feel, and it never occurred to me that there were boundaries to consider.

Then there were my sisters, who had their own range of outspoken to shy; self-assured to self-conscious. I wanted to be like all of them on any given day; and they, and all of their friends, contributed to my worldview of the ways that boys and girls acted around each other, and raised so many more questions about male-female relationships. With a family so large, with so many differing points of view at the dinner table, I'd become fascinated by human nature in general, what drives people and causes them to behave the way they do, how they relate to each other, and then mixing all that with the burning question of every confused, God-fearing child: *how can we all be so different if we were all made in God's image?*

Perhaps I should have gone out and gotten a sociology or theology degree or something to study this, but no; in my own way, I've been studying and conducting experiments by myself to help me develop my thoughts on how the Universe seems to work out those questions.

This book is the result of taking chance encounters with strangers and watching them turn into spontaneous relationships, and becoming an observer of my own unabashedly extreme curiosity to see if it serves a purpose. I'm a student of life, and in my own personal lab, I've discovered that my views have changed considerably from the mores of the masses—and from the masses I attended for so many years in the hopes of getting into heaven. At the end of the day, it's just Love that matters, but how we give it and how we receive it are not always the same, in form or function or ritual; and that little discovery is what set me on this big adventure I continue to live every day, right here in the suburbs.

On the one hand, I am a hopeless romantic; on the other, an intentional wild child. Now, let me try to connect the dots that brought me to this intersection.

Chapter 1

Downward Spiral into the Pit of Despair

The story begins in a decidedly depressed state of my own mind, the likes of which I wish never to return; yet in order to add context to my motivation and behavior, I reluctantly set the stage:

X and I had been married for over ten incredible years. He was one of those guys that everyone at a party works their way around the room to talk to before he disappears, always early, before the lampshades came out. He was full of wit, charm, knowledge, and integrity. I have absolutely no idea how I landed him after that fateful day when we were introduced by my boss. Our eyes met for about thirty seconds as we stumbled through introductions, classic love at first sight. The following day, I announced to my colleagues that I was going to marry that man, whose name I had already forgotten. My boss laughed and said, "I don't think so." It must have been fate, because two years later when X asked my father for my hand in marriage, Dad laughed and said, "If you think she'll say yes, go for it." My family loved him, surprised that I connected to such a funny, generous, stable man.

In any case, our life from the outside looked pretty sweet. On paper, it was a dream come true. I had the life I imagine people imagine. X had an unexpectedly explosive career in the entertainment industry, which gave us access to all kinds of red carpet events, sports, music, VIP badges in Times Square on countless New Years' Eves. We hung out with celebrities and didn't go anywhere unless there was a velvet rope separating us from the regular people. It was ridiculously A-List, and even now I cannot think of a single thing to complain about that isn't entirely superficial.

We had agreed that when we had children, they would have a stay-at-home parent, which would be me, since we were traditional at heart, and because X was in high demand, and I couldn't keep a job at my comparatively lower level in the industry. So we moved to the leafy suburbs, and I became a stay-at-home mom, queen of school volunteers, organizer of committees, thrower of parties, and biggest supporter of my husband's every move.

We had our babies, we strolled along the tree-lined streets, we waved to the neighbors. And as my husband worked harder, I went to playdates, and mommy-and-me classes, and nursery school. He worked some more; I renovated the house. He traveled some more; I made birthday cakes. He kept going, progressing in his career, everyone wanting a piece of him; I just got caught swirling in the eddy, faster and faster, going nowhere.

Don't get me wrong. I loved my kids, my home, and my husband. I wasn't quite so depressed (yet) that I couldn't see. In fact, I could see so clearly all the wonder that made my heart swell with joy on occasion, yet there was a deep, ungracious hole inside of me that was swallowing these moments before I could fully appreciate them.

Cut to the ten-plus year mark, when career promotions are the priority, travel is a regularity, kids are the overwhelming majority, and marriage—what's that? After our third son was born, *healthy-thank-God,* by Cesarean section after weeks of anxiety over both his and my health, my world came to a shattering halt. Post-partum depression, fueled by my absentee husband, more kids than I could feed at once, recovery time I didn't have, and my closest family too many miles away, set in faster than a fog over the harbor. I was drowning and I couldn't see the lighthouse.

I know this isn't unique. I'm guessing millions of women, certainly thousands more than are willing to admit it, go through this every year. Yet it's not an easy task to admit to depression in our society; less so in an upper-middle-class neighborhood, where one should be thankful for one's blessings and all the resources at one's disposal. Oh, the irony. So I stayed quiet and hired a babysitter to come for a couple of days a week, which nearly killed me because I was a stay-at-home mom! What good was I if I needed to call for backup? This thought alone would command most of my time in therapy over the next few years.

The days were excruciatingly long. I let the babysitter, an older woman who was happy to be needed, take over whenever possible. She cuddled my boys, fed them, drove them to preschool, took them shopping, bought them ice cream, and let people think she was Grandma. And I retreated, waiting for X to come home, not understanding any of these feelings that made me unwilling to participate in my own life.

You know when you take the dare and you realize, in the middle of it, you've made a horrible mistake? I dared to have three kids, and I dared to give them the "best" of everything, just like our parents wanted for X and me. The mistake was thinking I could do it. Not all of it; *any* of it. The depression had finally consumed me. What a failure I'd been, to think I could be a mom without my own mother, who'd passed away before I was married, to lean on for guidance. It was an agonizing, constantly-open wound, to realize I'd shortchanged my own children. They didn't need Disney World or every damned *Cars* character in a collector's Hot Wheels case; they needed a family unit that loved them, above all else, and I was too depressed to feel anything. And Dad was away, again. All they had was a babysitter and a satellite dish. It was these moments of utter, debilitating failure that I simply could not overcome.

Chapter 2

Lost in the Darkness

ife was moving very quickly in slow motion. The kids needed to be attended to *right now,* but the days took *forever* to end so I could go back to bed. I didn't see the depression for what it really was, and I'd underestimated this formidable opponent. I really thought I could fix it, or my husband's next promotion would fix it, or Mickey Mouse would fix it, but I never even saw how huge the sinkhole inside me had become, until perhaps that day when I snapped at my husband for forgetting that I don't like roses when he sent me flowers unexpectedly, for no real reason. He mentioned off-handedly that maybe the babysitter could come for a few extra hours each week so I could take a walk and get some fresh air.

That bought us some time for a while, my poor husband happily volunteering to do the night shift in the nursery, simultaneously trying to placate and avoid me. But eventually, the sleep-deprived months began to take their toll, so I couldn't even tell you when X started sleeping in his office, or on the floor of the nursery, or on the couch; but I do remember that most mornings when I woke up there was usually a small child in the space where he used to lay.

The baby was talking in complete sentences by the time my concerned but relentless friend, Dana, got me to agree to meet her for lunch in the city. It took me about two hours to get dressed that day, and that was only to come up with a top and a bottom that I could fit into, that didn't have those damned maternity labels mocking me.

"I thought we could go see Bill," Dana said breezily, referring to a holistic healer I had once recommended to her. I shrugged my shoulders and followed her into the tranquility of the office, with its waterfall rhythmically cascading down the interior wall.

After performing a pathetic series of muscle tests until I cried, Bill finally suggested I get a brain scan. I was too tired and weepy to ask him what that was, or to commit to *one more thing,* so I simply nodded and left. Dana took my hand and walked me to a café across the street, where she ordered us lunch and ever-so-gently, but forcefully, suggested it was time to give in to therapy, and even scarier, the possibility of mood-enhancing drugs.

"Honey, if you have a headache, you take a Tylenol," she said as I balked at the very idea of anti-depressants, as if they were still only given in asylums. "It's time for you to get better." Her one-woman intervention was so moving that I actually made an appointment for psychotherapy that day. And which I cancelled three times in three months, after noting the local address of the therapist. I mean, what if I ran into this hearer of all my sins at the grocery store? What if she knows my friends or neighbors? There were so many things to consider. Finally, even I had to admit that brushing my teeth was getting to be a chore. On the day that I finally showed up, I told the therapist that I had no idea why I was there, but that I didn't wear my seatbelt on the way over.

Fifty minutes later, she interrupted me: "We have to stop now, but if you're game, we can pick this up next week."

Come back? *Hell yes, thank you. I would love to come back next week!*

There is something to be said for being able to hear yourself talk without being interrupted by a two-year-old saying *mommy mommy mommy look mommy watch mommy mommy are you looking?*

Therapy turned out to be the highlight of my week. I simply could not believe it could feel so good to speak in uninterrupted sentences, and have the person to whom I was speaking nod along with everything I said, never making a judgment, never offering up a *what you should do is….* I could have said *karaoke* over and over, and she would have nodded, and I would have felt better.

In a state of depression, though, all good things come to a screeching halt at some point. Mine came when, once I was hooked on this talking thing, my therapist directed the chatter toward the harrowing decision to go on an SSRI. Talk therapy was like having a personal cheerleader; but anti-depressant medication meant there was really something wrong with me, and it just felt like I was giving up. I deflected it until I could not get Dana's words out of my head: "Honey, get rid of the headache."

My therapist referred me to a psychiatrist, who chose a drug that made sense, I suppose, on paper, but was just awful. She had to be getting a kickback from the drug company, that's how bad it was, but I can't prove it because my detective skills were busy trying to locate my soul. Not that I want you to be paranoid about consulting a doctor if you're considering the same move; all I'm saying is, don't give up if the first one sucks. Because this one *sucked*. After three weeks, I finally had to question her decision. I was gaining weight, and I was tired all the time. How was this supposed to help? "It'll calm you down so you can get some restful sleep," came the lame reply, "and when you're rested, we'll supplement your energy." Um. Okay but…When do I get to be *happy?*

Two months later, none the better except for my weekly hour of talk therapy, I ran into a friend who had just had a baby after significant challenges of her own. She was bubbling like a champagne bottle.

"What's in your Cheerios?" I asked her.

"Celexa!" she replied, as though she was the drug's gorgeous new spokesmodel, and I went screaming to my doctor: I WANT THAT!

Chapter 3

How X Came to Be

After months of isolation and struggle, I now had in my favor some key elements in my recovery effort: a team of support, which included the babysitter to care for my children while I worked on getting better; my new therapist, who listened to everything I said without whining; and my chiropractor, who hugged me every time I walked into her office, always knowing, but never forcing my limits. I also had my coveted bottle of Celexa and a new determination to justify all of it. I didn't come all this way for people to shake their heads at my coffin and say, *oh, what a sad story, poor girl....*

I was exhausted, but everything was in its place. I had three beautiful kids, a successful husband, a lovely home, and an army of helpers. Now what? I was functional, but not exactly happy. I had become, to put it lightly, a frump, sporting the ole baby weight as I introduced chicken fingers and pizza to the kids in an effort to keep up with the preschool playdate set; wearing drawstring pants and my husband's oversized sweatshirts to hide my still distended belly; my hair in a perpetual ponytail to minimize the forces necessary to comb it; and makeup simply didn't make the list. Yet, amidst all the things that I still had to show up for, like birthday parties and school parades—the irony of having to force myself to celebrate!—I felt like if I didn't yell at any small children for a whole day, I was a success.

While it's true that I wasn't so sad anymore, I found that the antidepressants delivered exactly—and only exactly—what they promised: mood stabilization. I never got beyond "not sad," and I still hated everything, all the time. I hated the school drop-offs and pick-ups. I hated the country club. I hated play-dates. I hated my husband for working all the time. It wasn't a venomous hate; it was a stabilized, slow-rising hate that was in my gut, right in front of my soul, where the Celexa couldn't kill it. I hated taking pills just so I could see clearly all the things that I hated, and I finally realized that if I was ever going to be happy again, it was going to be up to me, not an endless pre-scription. If I was going to be on medication, it was going to be temporary, and as soon as I was taking showers on a regular basis, I made a vow to take on the job of really getting better. I didn't know how I was going to do it, but I knew that if I could see that much, I had to be headed in the right direction.

I forced myself to exercise. I read somewhere that twenty minutes a day was the amount of time it took to activate the endorphins and make any fitness progress, so each day after I dropped off the kids at school, I took the baby in the stroller, and walked around the park for exactly twenty minutes. Maybe it was the fresh air, maybe it was the iPod playlist that didn't have ditties about the alphabet, or maybe, just maybe, that endorphin thing really was true, but I felt pretty good by the end of the twenty minutes, as if I had, perhaps, accom-plished something.

My husband had noticed the change in my behavior, and was thrilled that between the meds to keep me stable, and the exercise that was getting me outside the house, he was able to make it from bedtime to breakfast with fewer impulses to call 911. Based on my results, he was amenable to couples therapy, but soon he was back to working late hours, traveling every week, and waiting to get sick for the weekends, when I counted on him for a break. It never occurred to me that he needed a break from living with me.

Before long, I was actually thinking thoughts beyond my slowly-clearing state of mind on my walks. And after a while, I began to see one thing very, very clearly: our marriage wasn't working out.

Our couples' therapist was a huge help. In two sessions, I learned that my husband was every bit as depressed as I; only he had to hold it together in order to keep his new job. His travel schedule was grueling, but not negotiable, and putting up with my breakdown was not something he was prepared to do right at that moment, and it didn't look like we would find an opening in his calendar anytime soon.

By the third visit, I had a powerful feeling in my tightly-wound stomach. I turned to my husband and said, "This is too hard." He looked at me, nodded, unable to speak, but telling me volumes. We got up, shook the therapist's hand, and left.

It wasn't that we were unwilling to try to save the marriage. It was a knowing that it wasn't meant to continue. After nearly fifteen years of what seemed like a whirlwind, and now in different states of our own depressions, we were like two drowning victims trying to hold on to each other. Rather than sink together, we knew that it would be best to swim our separate ways and hope for rescue. And so my husband, now

X, began the search for an apartment, and my story began to unfold…

Chapter 4

Digging Out

As X was moving out, we agreed that whatever happened between the two of us, the kids would come first. It was the sigh of relief we both needed, allowing us to defer the mourning of our severed union for a bit, and redirect any energy we still had left into something positive that we could agree on.

We immediately brought our older child, who was on to us ("Why don't we pick Daddy up from the train anymore?"), to see a child psychologist. He responded so positively that we thought, *Why not make it fun for the whole family?* And eventually the middle child joined the ranks of psychoanalysis as well. Therapy seemed to be the one thing we all had in common.

By turns, I cringed, I laughed, and I gave great thanks that our broken little family had, among the four of us, seven therapy sessions each week. Each of us had individual sessions—with X and me two each, to monitor our respective SSRI meds—and in addition, we had a parental de-briefing session on the kids' sessions and what they meant. Counting travel time and ice cream or pizza afterward, we were looking at close to twenty hours per week devoted to therapy. That was the laughable part that made me cringe. The gratitude came in the blessing of being able to afford it, because if it hadn't been for all of those well-trained listeners who knew how to fill out insurance claim forms, we would have had no place to begin, and all of our therapists were enormously helpful in sorting us out and moving us forward.

I spent an early session working through the disturbing fact that I was having dreams about the kids' therapist, making it difficult to meet with him. My own counselor explained that this was not unusual, that it was perfectly within the normal window to fantasize about the first trustworthy male who comes into the kids' lives in the wake of uncertainty after a father moves out. It's more a fantasy about stability than lust, she explained, and I was glad that, as embarrassing as it was, I had brought it up. With that worrisome thought out of my way, I let my mind wander at night into strange territory:

I'm sorry, Mrs. X, but I cannot treat your child anymore.

Why not? You're the best child psychologist in the state, the only one I trust!

I've developed a moral dilemma. I'm in love with you.

I began to dress provocatively for my appointments with him—provocative meaning clothes without elastic waistbands and shoes that didn't have cushioned insoles—to see if I could get any reaction from him, secure in knowing it wouldn't go anywhere. Sad, maybe, but when you wake up after so much failure and misery, and look at all the work you have to put in just to make it through a day, and then realize that nobody's slept in your bed for a while, and it's not going to happen while you're lugging kids around in a minivan, you look for attention anywhere you can get it.

Fortunately, he was a professional; but he smiled just enough during our sessions—imagined or not—to make me feel like I was worth some attention. With that glimmer of acknowledgment, I called my girlfriend, Cattarina, who had been waiting for the signal. She was only too happy to take me shopping for some real clothes, and the makeover effort began, with the goal of making me look presentable on a regular basis. It wasn't long before I began to see the purpose to all those hours in the park. I even began to run a little bit, hoping to literally speed up the process. It was a victory of sorts for me, in baby steps, but forward progress nonetheless.

Meanwhile, X took his sports car and moved into an expensive, big-city rental apartment with views to die for, along with a monthly price tag that was more than our mortgage, car, and grocery expenses combined, in the suburbs. When I added it up one day, fully expecting to faint from the shock of it all, or at least have an excuse to be angry with him, something weird happened: I felt a wave of something that I can only describe as relief. *We have enough.* Perhaps this was the rainy day that we'd been saving for all these years, and it was I who had managed the checkbook all this time, I who had kept our budget modest, I who had kept us out of debt and within our means. We were able to afford this catastrophe because of *my efforts.* It was a stretch, I admit, but I patted myself on the back, anyway, for the first time since I don't know when, and I wrote X a card saying how much I appreciated his efforts as well. After all, he was going through the same shit, except he had to hold it together at work. How could I even consider being angry with him? It was funny, the cycle: maybe if he hadn't worked so hard, we wouldn't need this much money to cover all these expenses that resulted in our separation from his working so hard.

In any case, the realization was there that although this was an expensive process, we could manage it financially. We can do this. I can do this. Another victory. Things were starting to look up.

Chapter 5

Turnpike Steve

E arly in January, my sister called to invite me to a very small, private birthday dinner for her husband. She had reserved the chef's table at his favorite restaurant, and had asked me to join the exclusive party. I'm not sure if it was a pity invitation or not, but she definitely knew I could use a night out, which meant a weekend off, since she lived four hours away. I was so excited to have an excuse to get away from my own drama, and amazed that someone still wanted my company, that I called Cattarina to help me put together an outfit, and arranged to bring the kids to X for the weekend, which also included trading my minivan for his sports car. I readjusted the seat and mirrors, and took off down the interstate without looking back.

It was a snowy day, and people were driving badly, but amidst all the traffic, there was one car that stood out. It was the same make and model as mine, except with fully, tinted windows, and a license plate from the state in which my sister lived. As if separated at birth, the car held the same natural speed as mine, cruised in my lane, and maneuvered around other cars exactly as I did. I knew we were in strategic alignment when we went through adjoining toll booths at exactly the same time, and fell into sync again as we sped up on the other side. I didn't even feel like I was driving, but rather like the two cars were on a playdate, dancing along the snowy interstate as if they were filming a commercial.

I figured all I had to do was keep pace with this car; after all, its license plate told me we were going to the same destination, so I took it as a welcome sign from the Universe to just chill out and enjoy the trip. With my favorite music now at full volume, my brain relaxed from the stresses of where I'd come from, I took my gas and brake cues from my new driving buddy, and settled in for the ride.

Things were going great for a couple of hours when, once we crossed over into our destination state, my partner began to slow down, drop back in the lane next to me, and instead of leading the way through traffic, steadied alongside of me. It was only at this point, after a whole morning of compatible driving, that it occurred to me that this was not a teenage girl on her way back to college, nor a NASCAR hopeful, but a man. A man who was trying to flirt with me through tinted windows on a snowy January day after three hours on the turnpike.

Could there be a worse judge of character? Did he not realize that (a) I cannot see if he's smiling at me; and (b) he's trying to pick up a stranger full of antidepressants on a deadline? I had to laugh. Either he was a desperate freak, or I don't look as bad as I—no, it's the first one.

I couldn't stop smiling now; he had, after all, done all the driver work to get me this far. But I was annoyed by the late-game revelation; he'd had all this time to make his move, and he chose now, when we were this close to my sister's house? I didn't have time for this. After a few failed attempts to get him back in line, I scribbled my cellphone number on a piece of paper and held it to the passenger window until the phone began to buzz.

I picked it up. "Do you want to flirt, or do you want to drive?" I asked.

"Hello?" He asked. Not exactly quick-witted, but all I needed was for him to keep his pace. I would show some patience.

"What is your name?" I tried again, more politely.

"Steve," he said. "What's yours?"

"Steve? Honey, listen. I'm not going to be on this road much longer, so let's make the most of our time together. Drive like you mean it."

Steve was clearly taken aback by my conversational skills, but intrigued enough to stay on the line, and I was willing to engage him so that he would be distracted just enough to drift back into his heretofore underappreciated driving state. In the five minutes that followed, I learned where he lived, what he did for a living, and that…he took the next exit, something I was not expecting.

"Hey, where'd you go?" I asked as he disappeared behind a car-carrier and drifted a few lanes over, onto the ramp.

"Oh geez," he said, "I thought you were turning off. This is my exit."

"That's okay. My exit is coming up. I can take it from here. But…" I hesitated as I checked my rear-view mirror, and saw the state trooper behind me. "Steve, I have to hang up on you now. I think I'm about to get pulled over."

I hung up the phone, and checked the rear-view once more. Relief filled me as I concluded that the cop had made no effort to chase me down, and I was at my sister's house twenty minutes later.

And that's when the text came: Did you get a ticket?

I did a double-take, looking at the foreign number of the message's origin.

I smiled when I realized my driving buddy had been sweet enough to follow up. Then I realized I had given my phone number to a complete stranger, so I wrapped up my reply: No, but thank you for asking!

He didn't go easily. It took a few text exchanges to convince Turnpike Steve that I wouldn't accept his offer to pay for it, even if I had been issued a ticket for talking to him at the time. I brushed him off with Thanks for checking on me.

He tried another angle a few minutes later: When are you heading back?

Stop texting me! Or keep texting me? It was funny and weird and totally not normal. What was I thinking, giving my number to a stranger? But I kept answering, so what did that make me? Actually, sort of exhilarated.

After a few more exchanges about the differences in our driving schedules, I finally put my phone down after a Have a nice ride text, and prayed that he wasn't a freak who could hunt me down through my cellphone.

When I didn't receive any more texts, I figured it was all over with Turnpike Steve, and during the dinner party, we all had a laugh over the little episode, my brother-in-law admonishing me through a wicked smile that I should know better.

But truth be told, I was a little flattered, and had even become a little excited by the strange man in the cool car whose texts awaited me every time I picked up my phone that afternoon. Even a flirtatious freak was better than waiting for night to fall, so I could conjure up hopeless dreams about child therapists.

On Sunday, I got in my car to return home, and low and behold, another text: Wish I could drive back with you today. Maybe next time. Have a safe trip!

Oh, what the hell. Freak or no freak, he seemed harmless, and maybe even a little smitten, which my ego appreciated. I smiled to myself. *I've got a new buddy.*

And so it began. I pulled over to get gas after breaking out of a traffic jam, and returned the text: Wish there were more drivers like you today. Sunday drivers, ugh!

He quickly responded: Everyday drivers, ugh!

And again when I left the restroom: Are you sure your wife doesn't mind your texting during Sunday football? Sure it was a stretch, but what did I really know about this guy?

His response: I'm working today.

I didn't think that was an excuse, or even an answer, so I sat in my car for a few minutes while I texted him so. He didn't seem to understand that texting could be construed as cheating on his wife, but then again, he never said he had a wife, and anyway, I was just driving a car, for heaven's sake, so what did I care?

My thoughts wandered through this maze for the rest of the trip up the turnpike, spinning with every word, back and forth, freak or friend. If he was married and stupid enough to engage me, then it was his own fault, and I would alleviate myself of any guilt. Then again, what if he was single and wanted to start something with me? He might very well be an ax murderer, and I didn't even know what he looked like. Actually, I didn't really care. It was after all, the dead of winter. I needed something to distract me from the dreary, lonely days, and the kids' therapist was simply not an ideal choice for fantasy. In any case, Turnpike Steve was a welcome diversion from the lonely thoughts I had amassed in my head about my own life. Making up stories about him kept me busy for most of the ride home, and when I got back to my reality and swapped the car back for the minivan and the kids, I felt a bit more alive.

Monday and Tuesday came and went, and with another snow day shutting down school, I had nearly forgotten about Turnpike Steve when he checked in on Wednesday morning to let me know he was on the road.

I asked him how the roads and weather were going to be for his trip, and he shrugged it off. He was a commuter, he told me. It was part of the deal.

I texted: Why don't you just move here?

Because I work in both places.

Oh.

I pressed him further: But the weather...what if the roads are really bad?

They rarely cancel work. ;)

Steve worked in thoroughbred racing, and I told him I thought it was shameful to make the animals go out and race when humans need to sit by a warm fire and drink cocoa.

That sounds like a great alternative. Where do you live? Make me a cup and I'll join you. ;)

A flirt. Nobody's flirted with me in ages! I love to flirt.

I sent back: I can't reveal that information but maybe I'll meet you one day with...marshmallows or whipped cream? If work is ever cancelled, of course. ;) Who cares, right? I told myself. It's all in snowy-day, flirtatious fun.

Maybe I'll take off work if you tell me where you are!

Don't think so, buddy. You could be an ax murderer for all I know.

Too messy, he shot back. What would I do with the body? I like a clean car.

I was beginning to like Turnpike Steve. He had a sense of humor, and since he was a complete stranger, I had absolutely no responsibility for him, or to him. I almost didn't care if he was a married ax murderer-freak; he was light and fun; and just exactly what I needed to keep me from sliding backward and sinking under the weight of the winter.

Chapter 6

Lunchroom Revelation

t was loud in the lunchroom, all the kids talking and laughing at once, chatter I loved hearing. As I was helping them open juice boxes and finding spoons for their applesauce, I caught my child's eye across the room and smiled, just long enough to make it known that I was there.

I watched as the half-dozen other volunteer lunchroom parents stood over each of their children, not letting them participate in the lunchtime banter with the other kids, as if it were mommy-and-me time. I caught my son's eye once more, blew him a kiss and turned to go.

I thought about how different this school year was. Last year, before I'd admitted to myself that I needed help, I had been there every single day, like those helicopter parents back in the lunchroom, on call for everything—lunch, recess, pizza day, library day, committee meetings, field trips—anything to keep the depression from surfacing. It had been my lifeline. And my destruction.

I loved my children, of course. I was grateful that I had the means and opportunity, thanks to X, to be there for them, but as I walked down the steps of the schoolhouse, a thought hit me like a ton of bricks: I wasn't doing all of this for the kids. I was doing it to keep busy so I wouldn't jump out a window, sure; but really, I was making these efforts for the *other moms,* to show that I could be just as good as they were, just as helpful, just as "volunteery." I was falling apart, yes, and the breakup of my marriage and the disappearance of my husband was sure to be scrutinized, but I couldn't be a failure in the one thing I had left—mothering—if I was keeping up with them, right?

But I wasn't like them. I couldn't do this anymore. I was stable enough now to help my kids with homework, to welcome their friends over to play, and I could even help solve relationship problems for the elementary set; but slicing pizza and running after them on the playground just wasn't for me. I didn't fit in here, and it finally dawned on me that I didn't have to. There were plenty of parents willing to fill that role, and I didn't have to feel guilty about it anymore. I went home and made a note to ask the kids to choose a single volunteer activity for me, and then I would excuse myself from the rest, judgments and accusations be damned. The renegade thought of it lifted my spirits, and a new word popped into my head that stayed with me for the rest of the day: *Freedom.*

I sat down and sent X an email. Any remaining anger over his role in our crumbling situation dissolved within me, and I thanked him for being a wonderful and generous provider that enabled me to spend time at school and be involved with our kids on my terms. I told him that I hoped—and now I sincerely did—that he was feeling better these days, and that I would continue to work with him in any way to make our separation a success for all of us.

X emailed back almost immediately that my message couldn't have come at a better time. He was having a particularly rotten day at work, and the reminder that he could be appreciated, even as we were going through this awful time, meant a lot.

He can't stand to live with me, but I can still make his day.

And the most important thought of all came to me: *There was a reason I married this man, and just because it's not a fairy tale doesn't mean it has to be a horror story.* We can do this with civility and respect for one another. We can do this. We will do this. This is exactly what we are going to do. Perhaps we are both feeling free today. Another check in the "win" column.

Turnpike Steve texted later that evening: How was your day?

I was with the kids, about to tuck them in, feeling buoyant. Great as usual. Hey, what's down the turnpike, your mother or your wife?

Both.

I was taken aback by his unflinching honesty, but not surprised by his response. I half expected him to declare a mistress when I texted: Anybody up here?

Just you. ;)

Then he added: But I don't even know you, and you won't meet me.

And now I can't, I sent back, my heart sinking a bit, because now I know you're a married dog.

Why not? We're just text friends.

Unless we meet for a drink, dog. ;)

You won't try anything, you don't know what I look like, remember?

Yeah but I don't know about you.

I know you're cute. What do you think of me so far? He asked.

Was he kidding? I replied wearily: I try not to judge people.

You just did. You called me a dog because I'm married and texting you.

I couldn't argue that point, so I suggested that since it was late, we leave it for both of us to think about, and wished him a good night, certain that since there was no turning back from this new information, my winter fun had ended before it began.

As I predicted, I didn't hear from him at all the next day, and after a long, slow, week of unconsciously missing his silly texts, and the ego boost that came with them, I stopped looking. I even turned off the ringer on my cellphone so the absence of the distinct chime of an incoming text wouldn't be so noticeable. He had honored my assessment, and he had respected my thoughts, and Turnpike Steve had gone quietly away. And I hated how quickly I fell back to that lonely place because I had judged him of unworthiness, when it was me who felt unworthy. Celexa ain't good enough to fix that, and now we were both being deprived of the few hours of joy we found in each other.

The following Thursday, though, the mailman delivered a cosmic joke that gave us the perfect opportunity for a do-over.

Hey, I texted Steve, just got a letter from the town. They say if I want to keep a dog, I need a permit. Should I apply? ;)

His reply was almost instantaneous. Does that mean you're thinking about keeping me?

Not sure. Do you shed?

And just like that, Turnpike Steve and I were back.

Over the next several weeks, Turnpike Steve established a regular pattern of texting me on his way to town, and in the evenings when he had finished his business dinners. We texted about sports histories and rivalries, teased each other about musical tastes, and allowed for mild flirtations as the mood dictated. Week after week, we reconnected right where we left off, outside of our routines, with no responsibility. We never met, yet I felt like I knew him intimately. He never mentioned his family, and he spoke very generally about his work, but he knew I understood the depth of the things about which he could not elaborate. I knew he was a very important business-man, yet I could tell by the speed of his return texts whether he was in a playful or serious mood; and he appreciated that I didn't need him for anything except light companionship; a smile here and there. I never gave him a single detail about my life, and he never asked. He enjoyed the mystery of the girl in the car and I played the part with a big goofy smile, neither of us concerned it would lead to anything more. We never spoke on the phone; everything we had to say was better digested in charming, winky face-littered bubbles.

Turnpike Steve was my first text love. I loved seeing his name pop up on the screen, and the accompanying *ding* on my phone that indicated someone, a man, even an unavail-able man, was thinking about me at that moment. I loved the feeling that outside my otherwise cold and lonely world of being newly-single in a community of perfectly intact fami-lies, where I felt so foreign and misunderstood, someone was happily affected by me and looked forward to whatever I had to offer, in turn bolstering my own spirits. And I loved that I had this mysterious little compartment in my life that nobody knew about, nor could possibly understand.

It wasn't exactly a relationship, but our texting lasted for a couple of months. Turnpike Steve made a brutally harsh win-ter bearable, even fun. But it wasn't just that. In my growing quest to discover my new world and the meaning of the people showing up in it, I struggled to find the reason for Turn-pike Steve. The temporary excitement couldn't have been the end result, could it?

And then one day, it hit me. Turnpike Steve taught me—no, conditioned me—to take the drama out of my life, to see all things in my life as a blessing. With him, I had no baggage. As far as Turnpike Steve was concerned, I had no kids, no X, no age—no details at all. I was a pretty girl in a car with a quick sense of humor. When I texted with him, I simply let the parts of my life that didn't make me sound utterly fantas-tic, disappear, leaving him with a mysterious, carefree woman who loved life and could talk sports. I think I actually glowed when I texted with him. I liked being a carefree woman who loved life.

When my Real Life with kids and responsibility inter-sected with my Awesome Life of texting Turnpike Steve, I began to invent a new language. Soon I had taken all the irri-tating details and monotony out of my daily discussions, and what was left was a new terminology that kept him (and every-one thereafter) guessing. Thus, "driving the carpool" became "going out with a bunch of people." Teacher conferences and back-to-school nights became "events," and the kids' sports schedules were "previous engagements." All of these routine obligations were presented in such a way as to confirm that my life was full and exciting and impossibly perfect just as it was. And I wasn't even lying.

When I presented myself simply, without the whining of the everyday *it's always somethings,* the result was that I was perceived as this incredible woman who had everything fig-ured out. And the truth was, the more I configured my new vernacular to accentuate the positives and leave the negatives out altogether, the more I felt like I *was* figuring it out; and I realized along the way that there were no problems for which I couldn't come up with a solution. I kept coming up with creative ways to deal with the last-minute twists of everyday life so they didn't seem like negatives. I even got the kids involved in this new process, asking them to restate "I don't like…" into "I'd much rather…".

It was a slow and subtle change, but it was monumental. I didn't realize it then, but it was the beginning of a true transformation in my life. It seeped so deeply into my core without my realizing it was happening, until the day when one of my kids, determined to be angry about something that happened at school, shouted at me, "I don't want to tell you, Mom, because somehow you'll turn it into a good thing, and I'm really mad!" I stared at him in disbelief until we both began to giggle, and I never did find out what the immediately-forgotten event at school was.

I was learning that drama is a choice, and with every text, I was leaving it further behind. I have Turnpike Steve to thank for that. I hope that he got as much out of our short, sweet, text affair, for which I will always be truly grateful to the man I never laid eyes on, but whom I deeply loved.

Chapter 7

Big Bald Billy

C ertain that the barometric pressure had more than a little to do with my state of mind, the gray and cloudy winter was taking its toll despite the success of Celexa's role in stabilizing my mood. One particularly lonely, snowy evening, somewhere in the middle of a running text conversation with my friend, Kali, while I was making dinner, she texted, I have someone for you.

Before I could text back, she followed up with: Someone to practice with. Get one under your belt. No strings, no drama, nice guy, single, your age, likes kids.

If he's all that, why is he single?

He's here working with the team, she answered, referring to her husband's business. Kali was married to Alex, a professional athlete, not all that uncommon in our neck of the woods of nice neighborhoods in close proximity to all of the metropolitan sports arenas.

He lives somewhere else, her text continued, can't believe I didn't think of it before. He asked about the cake you made for my birthday. Told Alex he could kiss whoever baked it. He's perfect and he'll be gone by the end of the season before anything long-term can occur.

Hmmm. This could be an interesting turn of events, I replied.

He's on his way over to pick up Alex for a team dinner. Can I give him your number?

Of course. Do I have to make him a cake?

Thirty minutes later, I received a text from an unknown number.

Hi, this is Billy, Kali & Alex's friend. Would it be okay to call later? She said some great things about you, and I can't wait to talk and find out for myself.

I confidently replied right away. Aren't you at a party? Don't text while you're out with other people. It will keep. Let's chat later.

He texted back a winky face and I put the phone down and finished putting away the dishes. Five minutes later, there was the familiar *ding* of a text.

My birthday's coming up. Will you make me a cake?

Already with the cake? Go back to your dinner.

I can be discreet and text you too, he texted.

You don't even know me.

I'd like to, after what Kali told me. ;)

What did Kali tell you?

I quickly texted Kali to tell her he made contact.

What did you tell him besides I made the cake?

Kali: I don't know. Just that you're single. And you have kids. He likes kids. Alex probably said something in the car.

Billy replied, Kali says you're a great friend and mom, which is a real turn on. And Alex said you're beautiful.

I texted Billy back, That doesn't sound like something Alex would say. Then I added: But nice to know you get turned on so easily. ;)

Billy spent much of the next three hours sending flirtatious texts, and in between bathing the kids, reading stories and tucking them in, I responded in kind. As with Turnpike

Steve, I had nothing to lose by exchanging a few texts. It seemed to have worked him up, because by the time Billy got home, he was only too anxious to call.

"Hi there. I've been dying to hear your voice," was his opener.

"Hi. Do all your friends know you were on a date with your cellphone tonight? What do I sound like, anyway?"

"Pretty damn sexy; and no, I told you, I'm discreet," he replied.

"I like the sound of that," I teased.

"And I like a woman who can appreciate that."

"So," I ventured. "Let's clear this confusion up. What did our friends really tell you about me? I don't want to start off with unrealistic expectations."

"Well, let's see. Alex told me that your kids go to school together, and he told me you make great cakes. When I tasted the cake, I knew I could trust him when he said you're pretty hot."

"Oh, now it's 'hot,'" I giggled. "That sounds more like Alex's vocabulary, but out of context. Want to try again? What did Kali say?"

Billy took a deep breath. "Kali said that you are separated and need to be shown a good time, no strings attached."

"Ah, now we're getting somewhere," I laughed. "Let's go with Kali. She knows me better."

I could hear the smile and mischief in Billy's voice when he said, "You've got a great laugh. I like that. And I really like a woman who gets right to the point."

"Well, why not?" I said, braver than I felt. "Kali says you're far from home, and if we can offer each other something, I don't see the harm in that."

I wasn't sure if Billy was still on the line, because he didn't say anything for a long moment. But then I heard a sharp intake of air, and I knew he wasn't expecting me to get to the point *that* quickly. I tried to soften it a little and changed the subject.

"Where are you from, exactly?"

Billy and I talked about our backgrounds and our current states in life. Over nearly two hours, I learned about his hometown, his career, and his goals; and I shared very little about myself, only what I knew Kali and Alex would confirm. Before we said goodnight, Billy said, "I'd really like to meet you."

I told him that would be nice, but realistically I didn't expect too much, given what I knew from stories I'd heard from Alex about guys on the team—and also that the team was headed out on a multi-city road trip. I left it there, and suggested he give me a call when he returned. "Goodnight, Billy," I said. "Sleep tight."

After we hung up, he sent another text:

I really like your voice. You've got a great laugh. And now I really want some cake. ;)

I smiled to myself, and drifted off to sleep, a new adventure waiting to begin. Turnpike Steve was married and off-limits, but this one I could actually meet.

By the time we had agreed on a date over a week later, the snow had been piling up, and it looked as if it might be a questionable decision to meet in the small window of time in which our schedules intersected. Billy had been texting me every day while he was on the road, and I wasn't surprised when he began sexting, making provocative comments about what he imagined. I spent a lot of time giggling, imagining him in a hotel room with a roommate, trying to get worked up by a text from a girl he'd never met, and wondering if Alex knew. But I found him so disarmingly playful that I felt like a kid, and as I experimented with this bold new method of dating, I found myself with a growing ego and sexual desire to match.

We finally met at a popular steakhouse; one at which he was clearly a regular, as the maître d' showed us to a dark corner booth and brought us drinks without an order.

So this is how the team rolls. Billy motioned for me to sit, then scooted in as close as he could without sitting on my lap. He was huge, at least a foot taller than me, and had a giant, bald head that sat on an equally wide neck, a development that might have frightened me had Kali not warned me about it in advance. He looked at me without blinking and said, "I'd like to kiss you now, if you don't mind. Let's get it out of the way now, so it won't be awkward later."

He planted a soft kiss on my lips, and pulled away for a moment, presumably to make sure that I hadn't recoiled or snorted out a laugh. I smiled at his cheap offensive strategy, and he leaned in with more force, cradled the back of my head, and we kissed for more time than is necessary for two people who've just met.

"I feel like after all that texting, we're closer to our third date," he said, when he finally pulled away.

We ordered dinner, and talked at length about past relationships, their destruction, and what we were looking to rebuild in that department.

"Kali told me you want no strings attached. What, exactly, does that mean?" he asked, after a particularly sentimental story about his last girlfriend.

I decided that playing coy wasn't the best option. I had nothing to lose, and everything to gain by being direct.

"Listen," I said to Big Bald Billy," I'm still going through a separation. I'm not sure how it's going to turn out, but I'm a grown woman with needs. I can't wait for a finalized divorce and custody arrangements to start meeting them, and given those circumstances, I'm certainly not looking for another husband."

Big Bald Billy oddly enough, looked hurt. "So you're just eliminating the possibility that the right guy might be in front of you?" He quickly added, "or anywhere…?"

I cut him off. "I'm looking for an adventure," I told him. "I haven't had one in a long time, and I'm open to all the possibilities. But I'm not going into this or anything else with the idea that I'm coming out of it with a long-term commitment. If that's a problem, tell me now." He might be bigger than me, but I had control of the situation, and I wasn't going to hand it over. I could have been a deer in headlights, or the most confident woman in the world at that moment. I chose the latter and held his stare until he took a deep breath. *Here we go.*

Billy signaled for the waiter, waved off dessert and motioned for the check. "I'd like to show you where I live now. We can leave your car here."

I excused myself to visit the ladies' room, where I texted Kali the change in plans. If I was going to follow through on this bold persona I had going, I wanted her to know where I'd be in case it all went awry and my car was found still sitting in the parking lot.

We got to his house within minutes, although it was several miles away. He held the door for me, and then gave me a quick tour. "I didn't come to watch TV," I said after he pointed out the enormous flat-screen in the living room. *Why do guys always have to show off their big screens?*

We raced upstairs, horizontal within seconds, rolling around his bedroom with such ferocity you'd have thought we'd just been voted off separate islands after four months away from civilization. Big Bald Billy and I had no trouble working off the dinner and quite honestly could've had a couple of desserts. But it became clear soon enough that "getting one under my belt" meant: *big lead up, dazzling open, quick finish. One night only.*

Billy drove me back to my car, and kissed me one final time. "I hope you won't tell Kali about this," he said.

I had to laugh. "Why not?"

"Well," he said sheepishly, "she doesn't know this side of me, and I still want to be able to go over and play with the kids."

It was cute, the way he said it, but also very odd, so when Big Bald Billy didn't call or text the next day, I was disappointed, but not too surprised. He needed to get laid as much as I did, and that was the extent of it. After all, it was one under my belt, with no strings at all. I had achieved the intended goal, albeit much quicker than I'd expected. I was relieved on the one hand that we wouldn't be going through that awkward *yeah, I like you, too, but we're done here;* yet I was disappointed that he hadn't had the decency of a gentleman to follow up officially.

Sex is a funny thing; it has the power to create expectations. I finally figured out that the real reason I was disappointed was that although I had been adamant about my no-strings policy, the truth was that I wanted him to pursue me because I still needed the validation. I wasn't attracted to Billy, and that made it even worse: rejected by the rejected. I allowed myself some time to digest that, and then I refined my position. *Sex is just sex,* I told myself, *like burgers are just burgers.* I resolved to experiment with idea of sex for the sheer fun of it, the momentary freedom. That was the lesson I needed under my belt, and Billy had obliged.

Chapter 8

Adventures in Mexico

With the whole Billy thing behind me, and Turnpike Steve still married—there-but-not-there, and the end of winter nowhere in sight, I felt like I needed a vacation. So when X said he would like to take the kids for half of the upcoming winter break, I speed-dialed the travel agent and told her I'd like to book a weekend at the Caribbean spa she had sent X and me to a few years back.

"Haha, oh my, you're funny," she snickered. "Did you know that winter break is next weekend? The Caribbean's all sold out. How about Cancún?"

"The spring break place? No, thank you. I'll check out some other options on my own. I have a hard time believing the *entire Caribbean* is sold out."

Apparently there is a distinct disparity between supply and demand in the Caribbean in February. If I found a flight, I couldn't find a room; and if I found a place to stay, they didn't take Amex. It was exasperating. Finally, I called the travel agent back. "I give up. I guess I'm going to Cancún."

"Oh goody!" she squealed. "You're gonna love it! All-inclusive, you can't go wrong," she said, and I knew instantly that she'd just won herself a free trip to somewhere better than she was sending me from some kind of travel agent contest. "And don't worry," she added, "it's adults only, so I don't think you need to worry about the college crowds."

I was booked, and I told myself this was an adventure waiting to happen. I went up into the attic and brought down the three pieces of summer clothing that I could fit into and I was packed. I went to the store and bought all the ingredients for the juice cleanse I had been wanting to try, and then all I had to do was wait ten days for the flight.

The next day I invited Cattarina, my first "mom friend" who had most recently become my makeover stylist, to lunch. I proudly told her I had booked my vacation, but she was less than enthusiastic.

"Why aren't you coming with us?" she demanded. Every year, she and her children spent winter break with family on the beaches of South America, and they had been trying to include me for the past couple of years, trying to intervene in my depression spiral, but I had chosen depression. I'm brilliant that way.

"Because X can only take the kids for a few days," was all I could manage.

"Bring the kids with you!" She countered.

Um. No.

Eventually, she came around, and she even let me borrow the summer frock that I would never return and which would come to be known as the Magic Dress. It was a cute little pink and brown and white sundress that made me look like a tri-ple-decker ice cream scoop, and maybe that's why men drooled over it; nevertheless I was happy to have it as part of my grow-ing collection of complimentary clothing. I also unearthed a bikini that, thanks to my dedication to the cleanse program, I finally felt bold enough to wear. I was really ready to go, and now I was looking forward to my adventure in Cancún.

Turnpike Steve checked in the following Wednesday, the day before I left. He seemed busy.

You need an adventure, I texted.

Don't we all. I'm always working.

Ah, c'mon, you got a passport?

I can't get a day off, and you want me to leave the country?

You can be back by Saturday, I promised.

Where are we off to?

Not much of an adventure if I told you, I texted, and left him to do his very important work for the rest of the day. Poor Turnpike Steve, he never got a break.

The next morning I texted him from the airport. There's still time. Flight 4933 doesn't leave until 1pm, I teased.

He LOL'd me and I knew he was busy, so I forgot about him and boarded my flight. But he had been curious. He looked up the flight, and upon my arrival, I received his text: *"Tiene una buenas vacaciones, Bella,"* which sounded sweet, whatever it meant, but he definitely knew I was in Mexico. And he was probably thinking about me in a bikini.

The resort was beautiful. Totally sheltered from the rest of the world by vines climbing up ginormous walls around most of it. Mexican flames and morning glories, deep green strings of leaves balancing budding flowers, rising up taller than my house and stretching longer than my street back home, and the ocean surrounding the rest of it with blues of every shade, melting into the horizon. Only the playful, teasing rain clouds gave a hint that it didn't go on into another dimension. It was a lush and private compound, with a spa, a million different ethnic restaurants, and several pools, all with swim-up bars.

I learned very quickly that "adults only" is vacation speak for "weddings and couples," and I was out of practice with the language. There wasn't a single person on the premises who wasn't fused to another, with the exception of the check-in clerk. *Adventure is definitely going to be a challenge in this place,* I thought, as I muttered a curse on the travel agent and slipped into Cattarina's dress for my self-guided tour of the property.

I immediately signed up for a Mayan ruins tour leaving on Saturday, which would give me time to relax on the beach the next day, and still have time to explore the possibility of adventure that I came for.

I worked my way around the resort, checking out the wildly manicured gardens, the private, pristine beach, and the luxuriously indulgent spa. I was making my way back to my room, just past the last hot tub, tucked in beyond the last of the swim-up bars, when I heard the howling.

I followed the sound, and my eyes came to rest upon six people stuffed in a Jacuzzi littered with empty glasses of all sizes. The howling was coming from one of the guys in the Jacuzzi who was trying to get my attention. Not exactly to chat me up as much as point to a cocktail he couldn't reach on his own, and hoping I would oblige.

I handed him the hurricane glass and sat down on the edge of the hot tub. "Well, it looks like you all found Happy Hour," I said.

He eagerly took it from me, looked me up and down, and winked. I couldn't be sure if it was the alcohol or the Magic Dress, but I was delighted that he approved, and I relaxed a little more as they tried to make conversation.

I soon learned that the group was made up of three couples from Pittsburgh, all childhood sweethearts, here in Cancún to celebrate landmark birthdays. Or anniversaries. Whatever. They offered to summon the bartender so I could join them in a toast, but I politely declined. When they began to heckle me, I explained that I was almost finished with my cleanse and, as much as I enjoy a good time with strangers in hot tubs in foreign countries where I know nothing about sanitary regulations, I was going to stick to my plan. The bartender came to clean up the glasses and asked if I would like anything.

"Can you make a mango smoothie?" I asked, and when he brought the bright orange elixir on the double, refreshing and satisfying, I knew I'd be able to enjoy my four days here without sacrificing my cleanse victory.

Everyone in the hot tub was drunk. Ed, the one who'd motioned me over, and his wife, Patty, were the only ones who could still string words together to form sentences. After I told them I was in Cancún for the weekend by myself, they invited me to dinner with the gang.

"We'll show you a great time," Ed promised, and winked at me again. Definitely the Magic Dress. "Meet us at the central bar in an hour."

Chapter 9

Pittsburgh Ed

went back to my room and put on the low-cut, hot pink mini-dress that I had brought, and carefully balanced myself on my new five-inch suede sandals to practice walking. I thought I was coming for adventure, so I packed adventurous clothes. But tonight, since I was meeting couples for dinner, I just hoped I could pull off a casual *I'm sexy and I know it and I always dress this way* sort of vibe. I texted Cattarina, who had insisted I buy the shoes a couple of weeks earlier.

How the hell are you supposed to walk on these things? I pecked, as I tried to hold myself steady while I concentrated on the tiny keyboard.

Nobody said being hot was easy. Have fun!

I did my makeup the way she had shown me before my date with Big Bald Billy, but it was too much for the tropics, so I smudged it off and went with only mascara and lipstick. I felt good and, still hopeful that somewhere in this place there might be a widower that I missed, I headed out to the central bar.

Only two of the three couples from the Jacuzzi had made it, and Ed and Patty were still the only ones speaking coherently. We went off to find a restaurant where the five of us could hang out for a while, and we settled on a little Mexican bar that was completely empty and seemed as though we would each have our own exclusive waiter.

We sat at a high-top table big enough for six, with Ed and Patty on one side; me and the other couple on the other. We chatted for a while about nothing in particular, but it wasn't long before Patty had taken over in the story-telling department, and I felt a shoe brush over my foot, and hook under my sandal. I took a sip of my mango smoothie, and looked nonchalantly around the table. Ed was across from me, smiling. Another pass of his foot over mine, and a bigger grin followed.

Well. This wasn't what I was expecting, but I got game. I was all wound up and stuck at a couples' resort for the few days I had away from the kids. *Careful what you wish for, Birthday Boy,* I thought as I lifted my leg and jammed my Jimmy Choos between his thighs, never missing a beat in the conversation.

Pittsburgh Ed grabbed my ankle and then began to caress my leg, switching hands occasionally to grab a French fry off Patty's plate, and still managing to pull my leg closer to him. *He's good,* I thought. *And not in a good way.* At one point, he tried to hook my other leg simultaneously, but when I lurched in my chair, he swallowed his beer down the wrong pipe, dropped my leg, and asked loudly if the waiter could bring some water. I pushed my spike heel harder into his crotch as punishment, but he didn't take it that way.

When the group decided to sample another place for dessert, Patty took the reigns as designated leader, and made her way to the front of our pack. She took Ed's hand for a moment, but dropped it as she became focused on her mission. Ed dropped back, all the way behind me, and grabbed my ass, leaving his hand there for an uncomfortable amount of time. But hey, it was his risk, not mine—I was just trying to get a little excitement around there—and he was sort of cute, and I was feeling sexy, so I played along as if this sort of thing happened every time I walked out of my door. It was a trashy, yet liberating, behavior to test in my psychic lab. Was this what I had missed under my big brothers' protection all those years ago? It felt devilishly thrilling.

After they ordered a slice of apple pie, I realized the group had run out of things to offer by way of conversation. They had turned to discussing plans for a trip they had reserved for the next day, and I was getting tired of footsie. It wasn't like it was going anywhere. We'd had our little flirtation, but he had Patty, and I had a widower to find, so I excused myself as politely as I could.

"I've had such a fun time with you guys, thanks for inviting me out. I think I'm going to head over to the beach for a little walk and then go to bed. Goodnight."

It was Patty who spoke up. "We'll be gone all day tomorrow, but maybe we can meet at the pool on Saturday," she said hopefully.

"I think I'm signed up for an excursion on Saturday, but I'll look for you when I get back. Have fun tomorrow," I replied.

"Oh, I hope so," she said, "we're leaving on Sunday, and we'd love to hang out with you again."

Geez, Patty, let it go. I wanted to tell her that I didn't want to waste precious time with married drunks, and that I thought she ought to be worried about someone else instead of me.

"I'm sure we'll run into each other around the pool then. Goodnight, all." I took a nice walk around the resort and out to the beach. I slipped off my heels, laced my fingers through the straps, and sank my feet into the sand. It was a delicious feeling, and I took a few deep breaths as if to store the memory inside me. I looked up at the possibly-full moon and said a prayer of thanks that I was walking barefoot on a beach under the moonlight in February. Even alone, it felt incredible.

I went back to my room and got ready for bed. I hung up my dress, put away my sandals, and pulled on my royal blue, silk slip nightie, my absolute favorite piece of clothing. I looked out onto the patio, with its big, lounging couch and soft, comfy throw pillows, its private space defined by dense, low bushes and sporadic palm trees, beckoning me under the bright night sky. I grabbed my book and headed outside, sending up another little thank you prayer for the luxury of reading a real novel by the moonlight in my pjs, instead of *Goodnight, Moon* to the kids for the tenth time, back at home.

As I walked outside, I noticed what post-9/11 New York had trained me to identify as a suspicious character. It could have been a valet or a maintenance man, but all I saw was a shadowy figure lurking just beyond the palms with no props to justify being a hotel worker. I moved closer to the edge of my patio. The figure became clear.

"Ed?" I asked.

Pittsburgh Ed turned around and stuttered, "Um, hi, I…"

"What are you doing here?" I asked with great confusion, as I remembered Patty pointing to their room in a building all the way across the compound.

He fumbled for his words. "I was taking a walk on the beach…" and it became clear to me. This was not the way he planned this in his head, as the beach was a pretty decent distance away as well.

"You followed me, didn't you?"

"Yes," he said, sheepishly.

"Well, don't stand out there like a peeper, or someone will call security. Come over here."

He leaped over the bushes and landed on my patio, but once he saw that I was now wearing much less than what I'd had on earlier, he forgot his words again. "Um, I was just taking a walk…" he said again.

"No you weren't. You were looking for me."

"Yeah, I was."

"What do you want?"

"Um…you?"

"But your wife is waiting for you to celebrate," I said.

"She's probably not."

I know this looks bad from every angle. Ed was a drunken idiot, and I was as sober and as sexy as I'd ever thought I was going to be. I could have been responsible; instead, I was in charge. Why he wasn't with Patty at that moment was beyond anything I could guess—or really care about—but goddammit, I'd been working hard at this. I was exercising, cleansing, and sucking down antidepressants every damn day, and I finally get away…and this is my reward? He was sounding more and more like a seventh grader, so if this was supposed to be my big adventure—dammit—then let's have at it.

"Did you come here to kiss me?"

"Yeah."

"Then come over here," I directed him. It wasn't one of my better-known traits to be this bold with a man, but somehow the Universe gave me this one to practice on, so I got down-right bossy.

"I've never done anything like this before," he mumbled. *How adorable!*

"I'm sure you haven't. I'll bet that's why you're so good at footsie. I don't really care what you've done or not done before. You're here now, so you must really want me." I was more intrigued at that point with what *I* could get away with, so I relentlessly pushed to see where this was going to go.

He took a big step closer to me, so that there was only an inch between us. I looked up at him, a head taller than me, and he kissed me, pressing hard, but touching me only with his lips. His hands stayed at his sides, and when he began to sway, I was afraid he might collapse on me, so I pushed against his chest to steady him. He took the gesture as approval, and kissed me more urgently, now planting his hands on my hips.

What the hell. Here we go.

I pulled him onto the cushions, and we wrestled away the throw pillows underneath us. Taking the spaghetti straps off my shoulders, he began at my neck, and kissed his way south. He was very focused on his mission, and I remember looking up at the moon, thinking, *This feels nice,* and then, *There's no way he's never done this before.*

After a while, he unbuckled his pants and positioned himself on top of me.

"Aren't you forgetting something?" I asked. "Where's your condom?"

His face was a mix of arrogance and confusion. "Um, no, I told you I've never done this. Why would I need one? I never cheat on my wife."

I stifled my urge to laugh and said, instead, "And you won't be cheating on her tonight, my friend. Put your pants back on."

"What? But I'm here, and she's asleep and—can I just finish?" He pleaded.

"You can finish without me," I said, and I set about finding his missing garments. "Now that you're all worked up, go surprise Patty and thank her."

"Thank her? For what?"

"For being married to you," I said. I left out the being a dog part.

He began to pull on his clothes, when suddenly a thought occurred to him. "You're not going to tell her, are you?"

"Why would I do that? That would only ruin her vacation."

Pittsburgh Ed let out a sigh of remorseful relief. "I feel like such an asshole."

"Oh, Ed, honey. You only *feel* like an asshole because you didn't get to finish. You *are* an asshole because you started in the first place." I might have added that I was an asshole for telling him to hop over the bushes, for being perfectly okay with it—as long as he had protection—but I was in the middle of daring myself to be bold on this trip, and right now, I was the boss, despite my questionable wisdom. For reinforcement of my superiority, or at least to make myself feel better, I added, "I just want to make the clarification for you, so you won't be confused later when it happens again with someone else."

My confidence apparently made him very nervous, because he asked again, "Who are you going to tell?"

Now I was exasperated. "Listen, Ed," I began, "I'm single. I have nobody to answer to. So I can tell anyone I want, and I don't owe you, because you started this whole thing." It felt good to be a powerful, single woman. It's a role I don't think I'd ever played before, and I wanted to linger here, but I could see that this guy was really starting to sweat, and for a second I felt sorry for him, so I brought it home. "I don't have any interest in upsetting your wife or anyone else. She doesn't deserve that, and it's not my style, anyway. It's up to you whether she finds out, and if you're smart, you'll keep your mouth shut and start treating her like a queen while you still have the opportunity."

I thought I was making it clear to Pittsburgh Ed that by telling his wife about something that didn't even happen, with someone he didn't even know nor would ever run into again, he would ruin this vacation, and all vacations going forward, and future birthdays or anniversaries, and even the entire country of Mexico for her. But I'm sure he caved and told her anyway, because two days later I saw the whole gang at breakfast, and wasn't even invited to join them.

Chapter 10

Mayan Mischief

The 14-hour Mayan adventure began on Saturday with a 6 a.m. pickup in an empty 10-seat van. I was the only person from my resort on this excursion, and the driver said we had an hour to drive before the next pickup point. I had a tiny backpack with a water bottle and some raw almonds, but I'd had a smoothie before I left my room, so as much as I would have liked to have drifted back to sleep, I was wide awake and ready for anything. I took the seat behind the driver and we chatted about the tour.

An hour later, at the first stop, we picked up a mother-daughter duo who were trying to rebuild their relationship after an ugly divorce. They were "team building," the over-sharing mother told me, because she was the human resources director for a large firm and she sends employees on this sort of thing all the time, and results don't lie. The daughter, a teenager, rolled her eyes at everything her mother said, and I found myself hoping that she would get to live with her father. They sat behind me, but at the next stop, when we added three women who were cousins from Canada and a couple from India on their tenth anniversary, the team-builders squeezed in next to me. At the last resort stop, we picked up an unmarried couple, a beautiful young law student and her boyfriend, who was a firefighter. They were a stunning couple, but as they tried to find space together in the van, the firefighter, Sean, noticed that the passenger seat was empty, so he left lovely Gina in the back and buckled in up front.

I had a great view of the very handsome Sean. Young and built, he wasn't very talkative until I asked what kind of work was involved in being a firefighter. He regaled us with some exciting stories, incredulous facts and silly jokes, and I liked the simple, almost lazy way in which he spoke, even as the Team Mom kept mouthing *"He's dumb as a rock"* to me every time I took my eyes off him.

The day was long and active. The first activity was zip lining through the rainforest, or a reasonable facsimile thereof. I was alone, so much of the time I paired up with the Canadian cousins, but just as often, and mostly because it became clear that Gina was not there of her own volition, I found myself hiking with Sean. He was, it turned out, dumb as a rock, but I didn't care that he didn't know who the president was; I just kept steering the conversation toward firefighting, since all of his faculties were invested there. I had no doubt that if I needed to be rescued in any way, he was the guy to do it. When we paddled canoes through the lagoon, I positioned my boat alongside him; and when we walked up the steps to the Mayan temple, I was sure to climb just ahead of him, offering of course, to take photos of him and Gina wherever possible.

The grand finale was a Mayan cave, an underground spring created by time and nature that in its simplicity held all of us in awe. After the active day, we were ready to swim under the darkening, peaceful holy ground. The group prepared to work its way down the very steep path to the water, but by that time, Gina had had enough.

"You go," she commanded. "I'll wait here," and turned back to the guides waiting in the air-conditioned van. Sean didn't hesitate for a minute; he had been waiting all day for this.

The history and stories about the cave were fascinating, and while I wanted to ask more questions, I didn't want to waste time behind the curious crowd forming around our guide, so I took the liberty to swim around and explore on my own. Sean had the same idea, and when I beached myself on an underwater rock after floating quietly on my back for a while, I was startled to find him staring at me.

"It's so quiet down here," he said, never taking his eyes off mine.

"Yes," I agreed, "it's a perfect place to get lost."

"Hey, come over here." he said, suddenly animated. "Follow me!"

He led me around a giant boulder to a dark alcove. There, he took my hand and further snaked around through smaller clusters of rocks before stopping next to a deep, emerald-colored well.

"Let's go to the bottom," he said. "It's not too deep, but it's incredible."

For a minute, I thought he might try to drown me or something, but the combination of his twinkling eyes, coupled with his excited, child-like grin, disarmed me, and once again, I found myself being lured by a stranger.

"How deep is it?" I asked.

"Not very. Give me your hand." We took exaggerated breaths of air and descended beneath the surface. The bottom wasn't far, maybe nine feet or so, but the still, quiet echoes were indescribable. Eerie, serene, meditative. We resurfaced and grinned at each other, not saying a word, lest it break the spell, and with the next breath of air, he let go of my hand and moved it to my waist. Gently, he pulled me close, and we descended again, this time as a single unit, and as we sank to the bottom, and slowly rose back, the only thing I felt in the stillness were the alternate beats of our hearts in excitement. It was seductive, and we remained still, once more down to the bottom and back, and when we finally let go of our breath, it was too much.

We swam to a shallow, submerged rock, and began pawing at each other, fighting for breath and body as our lips refused to part, exploding just as we heard the guides calling for the group to account. It was intense, forbidden, and tranquil all at once, timeless in those few, powerful moments, and sent my heart and body into a simultaneous state of stillness even as it electrified me like a thunderbolt. It was a moment of pure, innocent bliss, like the spring itself, and in those few minutes, my appetite for adventure had been satiated.

We made our way to the steep ladder and he squeezed my hand one last time before handing me off to the guide, both of us back in reality, instinctively understanding that what had happened was some sort of sacred, spiritual experience. I followed the guide out of the cave, and didn't look back.

Chapter 11

Dating Journey

B y the time I was deposited at my resort, well after 8 p.m., I was so tired I could barely stand up. But I was only there for another day and a half, so I reasoned I could at least get dressed and sit at the bar with a smoothie.

I arrived at the bar wearing the other outfit I brought, a soft blue cocktail dress and some strappy sandals. I couldn't be bothered with the heels tonight, although it was worth noting that these sandals were still two inches higher than anything I'd worn during my marriage. X and I were the same height, so I always wore flats. Now, even a two-inch sandal made me feel sexier than I had in a decade.

The bartender was being kept busy by a couple of old guys who had just finished a round of golf, and were ready to make up the hours they'd missed at the open bar. I had been trying to get the bartender's attention for some time, and I was ready to give up when a good-looking guy, about my age, wedged himself between the two of them, and asked if he could order something for me.

A minute later, he handed me a smoothie, and I was just about to throw in some batted eyelashes along with my grateful smile when a pretty, petite blond girl sidled up to him.

"Okay, honey," she said to him. "I think I fixed it. They screwed up the reservation at the Japanese restaurant, so we're going to the Indian place instead." She looked at me and smiled with an outstretched hand. "Oh, hello. I'm Wendy."

"And I was just about to say I'm Jeff," said her honey and my bar hero. "Are you expecting someone?"

"No," I replied. "I'm embarrassed to admit that I didn't read the fine print that said this was the couples' capital of Cancún, so I'm here alone."

"Oh!" exclaimed Wendy. "That's so brave of you, traveling to a Mexican resort alone!" But the way she said it, it didn't sound condescending or even girlie. She really meant it. "We're here with Jeff's brother and his wife," she continued, as if she had planned on meeting me. "If they ever get here, we'd love to have you join us for dinner. We're going to the Indian place."

"Thanks," I said, wary of being the fifth wheel again. "I'd love to join you, but this is my dinner, right here. I've been traipsing around Mexico since 6 a.m., and this is about all I can muster."

"Nonsense," said Wendy. "You are dressed like a movie star, and you mustn't waste it. You're coming with us."

What is it about bossy American wives? I reluctantly agreed, mostly because I found Jeff to be attractive, and this seemed to be the trend, but I admonished myself and resolved to behave better this time.

It wasn't too long before Jeff's brother and his wife joined us, and we all walked over to the Indian restaurant. They were a gregarious group, full of laughter and no shenanigans. I really was having a wonderful time when I begged off after midnight, promising to look for them by the pool the next day.

I woke up on Sunday, headed to the café for some herbal tea and a smoothie, and eased myself into the day. My Mayan adventure yesterday was active enough to justify a leisurely day doing nothing but reading my book by the ocean. I gathered my stuff and headed out past the pool to find myself a beach lounger when I heard someone who looked like they were drowning, arms flailing, screaming my name from the pool.

It was Jamie, the brother's wife from last night, who hadn't had much to say except how "wild" it was that I'd come here alone. She called again, grabbing a thin, dark-haired young man, who was clearly as embarrassed as I was when she shouted, "Look! I found the only other single person here! It's fate!"

I smiled as gracefully as I could with a hundred pairs of eyes staring at me from all directions, and made my way to the edge of the pool so that she would stop screaming.

"This is Mark. He's from North Carolina, and he's here alone. We're all having dinner tonight, and that's that," she said by way of introduction. Another bossy American wife.

I composed myself and looked at her victim. "Hi Mark, it's nice to meet you. Perhaps we'll be engaged by the end of the night, and can put an end to the shame of being single in Cancún. I'll see you later." I smiled and excused myself in order to rest up for our epic date, and headed to the beach.

We were to meet at 8 p.m., and Jeff's brother and I were the first to arrive. Jamie had, not surprisingly, been drinking all day, and he wasn't sure it was a good idea to wake her for dinner. He was wickedly funny and easy-going, like Jeff, and I thought it was charming that they were best friends and vacationed together.

When our party was complete, we made our way to the Japanese restaurant, where Wendy was tying up negotiations for a private room. "It's an engagement party," I heard her say.

I looked at the new guy and said with a giggle, "I guess that's us," and I could tell he didn't get the joke fully, so I teased him some more. "Why so serious? It's your last night in Cancún. Relax, I won't bite."

Turns out, saying you're engaged at a couples resort in Mexico may even be better than celebrating a honeymoon. Maybe it's because everyone honeymoons in Cancún, but engagements mean repeat business with a larger group for the ensuing destination wedding, so even with the all-inclusive ticket, the service became over the top; our group was given endless top-shelf shots and extra servings of food from waiters who suddenly told jokes and danced, delivered plenty of desserts, and finally escorted us to the courtyard after dinner, where people were shooed out of front row tables so we could watch the band. They even took our photos.

"See what happens when Wendy plans an engagement?" I teased Mark again, "do you think she'll make our wedding this lovely?"

Mark looked away, and as I craned my neck to follow his gaze, intending to make a goofy expression to get him to liven up a bit, I saw that his face was completely contorted. As the band played *Wonderful Tonight*, the rest of our party got up to dance, and I asked him, "Are you okay?"

"I'm trying, I really am, but my marriage only broke up a few months ago. It still hurts."

"That's okay," I said reassuringly, not at all annoyed that I had spent the entire evening with the biggest single dud in the land. "Was this your wedding song?"

I had fully expected him to break down at the question, but instead he looked off into the night sky and shook his head. "Journey," he said, wistfully. "'Don't Stop Believing.' That was our song." I think he bit his lip to keep tears back as he said it.

I'm not one for all the traditional wedding stuff like throwing the carefully-selected bouquet or shoving perfectly good cake up your true love's nose; but a first dance to a timeless melody I find to be charming and romantic. So this one completely threw me for a loop. I stifled the laughter about to burst out of me as best I could, but the contrast of imagining a soulful Eric Clapton singing about his beautiful bride's every move, compared to the vision of mullet-headed Steve Perry singing with his fist to really, really hold onto that feeling was just too much. It took some effort, but I managed to say, "I'll get you some water," so I could excuse myself.

I went to the bar and dissolved in laughter at the thought of a bride-to-be accepting "Don't Stop Believing" out of all the other songs in the jukebox to confirm her marriage. Jeff came over, and asked what was going on.

"You set me up with Heartbreak Harry," I said.

"What are you talking about? And I didn't, Jamie did."

"Well then Jamie should have to sit with him and make him believe again."

"Believe what?" Jeff wanted to know.

I burst into laughter again as I told him, "His wedding song. Journey…" I couldn't get anymore out, I was in a fit of giggles.

"What's so funny? *Faithfully* is a popular wedding song."

"Don't. Stop…"

"Stop what? What is so damn funny?"

"Believing! 'Don't Stop Believing' was his wedding song!"

I shook my fist in the air.

Jeff caught the giggles with me and by the time his brother had joined us, we had to turn around with our backs to the band because we were laughing so hysterically we were shaking. Wendy was sitting with Mark, who had composed himself enough to make small talk.

Jeff and I punched each other until we could manage to appear more mature, and then we brought a round of drinks and water to the group and made a toast to new friends and new beginnings, and possibly an all-for-one, one-for-all cheer. I can't be sure. But with Mark a little more social than before, we headed to the disco.

In the dark of the strobe lights and house music, and with everyone except me a few drinks tipsier, we all hit the dance floor, intent on finishing out the evening on a high note. It wasn't to be.

Mark and I had taken a time out to rest, and as we chatted, I looked up and saw Jeff waving at me from across the bar. I waved back and he winked, and ten seconds later, the DJ request came on, and the brothers exploded in hysterics as "Don't Stop Believing" echoed throughout the dance hall. Mark got up without a word and headed toward the bathroom, and I picked up his beer bottle and threw it twenty feet across the room at the brothers, then went back to my room to pack.

Chapter 12

The Beginning of Something

t was the perfect way to leave Cancún. On the one hand, I had been in a beautiful resort and had some interesting experiences; on the other, it ended in such a way that I looked forward to going home. I had needed this break, this out-of-character break, so badly; but I missed my kids, and I needed to go back to the reality I knew. All this flirting, wild stuff was fun, and it jazzed me up in the confidence department, but it was all tinged with ickiness, and I wanted to leave it behind.

Sitting at the airport and in the immigration lines on the way home, I received lots of text photos from Wendy of our dinner at the Japanese restaurant. She must not have heard the whole story about Mark, and she'd had my cell number for making dinner arrangements, and now she was sharing the memories. I thought it was sweet, and as I looked closely at the photos, I could see the grief and fear in Mark's face, and although my heart sank for his sadness, I simply will never be able to hold a straight face if Journey ever comes on the radio again.

I got home, and X brought the kids over, but he didn't leave right away. We were still in the awkward, chilly stages of our separation, and kept our distance from one another. I had insisted that for the purposes of keeping our boundaries, and as not to send mixed signals to the kids, he should bring them to the back door, and not venture further into the house, so he just sort of lingered at the kitchen door. I had missed the boys so much. I just wanted to put us all in our pajamas and yes, read *Goodnight, Moon* with a new appreciation; but I couldn't tell if X was trolling to find out where I'd been, or if I was imagining him looking at me differently after the weekend I'd had.

After his first four days with the kids alone, he would be heading back to a quiet apartment. Was he happy or sad about it? I spoke as breezily as I could about how the resort was lovely and that I'd enjoyed the warm weather, but was glad to be back. X never understood the value of more than four days of vacation, so I added the last part for him. For what purpose, I didn't know. Old habits crept back as soon as a familiar opening was there, and I was trying to make him feel comfortable, as I'd always done. Only now, in *my* home, the house that he moved out of. I didn't know why, but I felt guilty that I'd had a good time.

When he finally left, I was completely exhausted and I'd changed my mind about snuggling in pjs; all I wanted to do was collapse into bed, but the kids were full of stories. Not really stories, as much as reports of their itinerary. They went to see Uncle Y, and Grandma, and Daddy's friends from college. It was then that I realized that poor X didn't know how to be with his kids without backup. I had been torturing myself for this shortcoming on a regular, ongoing basis, every time I sent them off with Grandma Sitter, but four days? It made me sad to think about it, for all of them.

I looked at the three little monkeys jumping on my bed and thought, *are kids resilient or what?* There they were, tiny creatures who relied on us grownups for every little thing in their lives. They studied us as we tried to figure things out for ourselves, and we would struggle, and they would watch, and we would give up, and they would keep playing, and we would get angry, and they would wait us out, and we never figured it out, and they snuggled up and loved us anyway. I so often felt like I didn't know what they needed. I had run away for a few days because I couldn't give them any more of me, and yet they only needed love. And the occasional juice box.

I was soothed by this revelation, happy to be with my children again, completely removed from the travel and back to the normal. We brushed our teeth and cuddled up for what I thought would be a quick nighty-night. And then all the kids wanted to do was account for every minute that I was not with them. They told me what they ate, which clothes they wore, what toys they played with, who was present. They were fully animated, and sleep was no longer on the agenda.

And I changed my mind, again. I wanted to go back. I was just so exhausted from my travels that I wanted to put them to sleep and shut my door for a day of recovery. I couldn't wait for them to be quiet. I had forgotten how loud it was in that house. I loved those little people with all my heart— didn't I just conclude that that was enough? But they'd been home for only an hour, and they were already driving me crazy again! Was I allowed to feel that way? After I'd missed them so much?

And then, as busy as they were, as talkative as they could be, as many questions as they could ask, they just turned on a dime and drifted off, slowly, quietly, angelically into a whole different realm from anything I could imagine. It was a serenity, a knowing, a sweetness that said, *It's okay, Mommy,* and before I could process any of it, there they were, snoring quietly and dreaming with that peaceful, perfect expression that takes my breath away.

My grandmother used to tease me: *You're a good kid...when you're asleep.* She used to laugh when she said it, but I finally understood what she meant. There, in the quiet of what used to be our lonely old house, there became a comforting calm in our new, still undefined *home.*

It's only the beginning, I told myself. *It's only the beginning of something I can't name, but I can feel it inside me.* That crazy, upside down, loud, chaotic existence was changing. That venom that had infected me with anger and frustration and depression and resentment was really retreating. A shift was occurring. It wouldn't be instantaneous, and it wouldn't announce itself, but it was happening. For the first time in what had been far too long, I felt really hopeful.

I had taken a vacation to another country alone. I did it all by myself, and now I knew that I had choices in my life. I could either curl up and wait for the kids to graduate, or I could start to make my life my own, even with the kids in my bed and their demands on my time. I realized that life comes in cycles. There are ups and there are downs. The time had come to shorten the down cycles and keep moving forward, toward the up cycles, and with a renewed resolve, I knew that soon, I would be able to do it even without the pills finally, all by myself. I could almost see the horizon.

I texted Kali to tell her that I was home safe, and that I felt new again.

She texted back: It's about time.

Chapter 13

Spring Break

The winter's bitterness began to thaw, and my four days in Cancún had shown me that I could do anything I wanted and get away with it. But what was I doing? I was grateful for the irregular regularity that was Turnpike Steve. He had become like a beacon in my world, for two days a week. My trip to Mexico coincided with his "away days," and I was glad he was still the same when I returned. However, he had been gearing up for spring, his busiest time of the year, so while he was still texting regularly, the messages became fewer during the days, and I was forced to find other things to do than wait around for his texts.

Fortunately for me, I had children. There was no end, really, to the amount of time and attention those little beings, perfect though they were, could demand. I was in a good place after my getaway, boosted in spirit by the sheer absurdity of the events that unfolded there, and so I was ready to give new energy to my boys. I began to take an interest in things like cooking again, but the ever reliable Grandma Sitter had been anticipating a breakdown from the get-go, and had been staying later and coming earlier over the last couple of months, picking up any slack I let out, and now she was reluctant to let me take the boys to their activities, insisting they had a "routine" of stopping for snacks and visiting her elderly neighbors. And routine is what kids need, yes?

Taking this all in, I decided I was so grateful for this woman, who had taken my children into her heart; she certainly loved them more than I could have ever imagined in my emotional absence. She was a gift to me, and my kids were a gift to her. I was getting stronger and feeling better, but I still had some work to do on myself, so I let Grandma Sitter continue her schedule with the kids, and that left me wondering what was next?

I took up yoga and made my way back to my friends. I agreed to another shopping spree, in which I was happy that Cattarina's philosophy of "less is more" meant I could still look good on a budget, and squeeze in a mani-pedi, too. I discovered things I could do on a daily basis that made me happier. In addition to getting dressed and well-groomed, I was exercising, reading, and writing. I even took up piano lessons along with the kids, and I practiced every day.

One Saturday morning, as X was transferring all of his stuff from his car to the minivan for his weekend with the kids, I held up my hands. "Stop," I said. "We can't keep doing this. You need a car that can handle the kids."

He agreed, but refused the idea of driving a minivan. He had his image to think about, after all.

"Fine," I said. "Let's go shopping."

X and I had never lived beyond our means; our cars were paid for, and we took good care of them, right up until they died. So when we went to the dealership about trading in his now-ancient car, classically sporty though it was, for its new SUV counterpart, which X decided was a perfect fusion of masculinity and kid-capable, we were nearly laughed out of the place.

"Just buy it. Don't even bother with the trade-in," I said.

"But shouldn't we think about it some more? It feels like I'm making an uninformed decision."

"Look, X," I reasoned, "you've had that sports car for a decade. It's a great car and still runs like a charm. But it's time to upgrade. You need the SUV for the kids. You love it, it feels good, and frankly," I said with a cockeyed grin, "it's a babe-magnet. It looks good on you. Buy it."

"But what will I do with the other car? I can't get two garage spaces in the city."

"I have a garage at the house," I found myself saying. "I'll keep it, and you know where to find it if you need it." I couldn't believe it felt so good to be this generous.

X thought that was a wonderful idea, and, just like that, I had a sports car.

Before I knew it, it was the kid's spring break, and X had them for the week, so I headed to our house up north to see about repairs. We had purchased the tiny vacation cottage on a lake just after we married, and the kids and I spent time there as a distraction while X traveled for work during the summer. He pulled up in his new SUV, outfitted with new booster seats, and I tossed my backpack into the sports car, and off we went in separate directions. With the projected forecast for spectacular weather, I was looking forward to the road-trip and hours of peaceful solitude.

The ride was wonderful. It was a beautiful sunny day, no traffic, and just me in the car, singing at the top of my lungs along with my iPod playlist. I was cruising and singing my way through the mountains when I noticed a white pickup truck on my tail in the left lane. I moved over to allow it to pass, and smiled at the driver as he took off ahead of me. A little while later, I found myself trailing him, and he made the same maneuver, only as I passed, he seemed to be scowling at me. *Geez*, I thought, *what's with the sour face?*

He followed me for a while until, somewhere on I-380 in Pennsylvania, he moved into the lane next to me and grinned, waving me off at the next exit.

I smiled as sweetly as I could, shook my head and waved goodbye. He exited at the next ramp, and I turned up the music and continued on, laughing to myself.

A full ten minutes later, as I approached the interchange through New York, the white truck reappeared, now with the driver smiling mischievously and waving his cellphone. I couldn't help but giggle. Had he actually gone off the interstate, only to come back to find me? I got the answer when he held up a piece of cardboard with his number on it. *This is crazy*, I thought. *Turnpike Steve, Part Two.*

Maneuvering through merging interstate tractor-trailer traffic while keeping a steady pace with him took a bit of finesse, and a sympathetic understanding of the new hands-free cellphone laws, but I finally got the numbers into the phone and hit send.

"I couldn't help it," he answered before I asked. "I knew I'd regret it if I didn't try."

"That is very flattering, 390," I said.

"390? What's that?" He asked.

"It's the interstate number. And the contact name I gave you as I dialed from your sign. Do you do that sort of thing often?"

"First," he said, laughing, "it's interstate three-*eighty*, and no, I just wrote that on the first thing I found while I was stopped on the ramp. You have a great smile, you know," he explained as he drew up alongside me and gave me an exaggerated goofy grin so I'd reciprocate.

I laughed. "Well, *first*," I countered, "you're *390* now. I'm not changing it, so you'll have to live with it for all eternity, or until we hang up, so get used to it."

"Fair enough," he said.

"And *secondly*…how long have you been so unhappily married that you have to find strange girls on *interstate 380* to flirt with like that?" *I've really got to find a more clever way to get this information if this is going to happen again,* I thought to myself.

"Sixteen very happy years, actually," he said plainly, and I blanched at his frankness.

"And how many kids, may I ask?"

"Four. A nice mix," he said without a hint of shame.

"And you are how old?"

"Forty. Just had my birthday last month," he said as proudly as my six-year old might have reported it.

"Let me get this straight. You're forty years old with a wife and four kids, and you chased down a complete stranger on the highway because you like my smile? What is this, a midlife crisis?"

"If you must know, it was your smile *and* your driving ability," he said, as if that was the recognition I was waiting for, and made everything else respectable.

"Oh, well then," I said. "I don't mean to sound like I'm not flattered or anything, but you're a dog." *C'mon, Universe, I already have Turnpike Steve and Cancún is behind me…*

"Oh, I love my wife," he said cheerily. "Sixteen years and I still want to have sex with her every time I look at her."

"Well that's more information than I need," I laughed. "So then what exactly, do you want from me?"

"I have no idea."

"Sure you do, 390. Go ahead and tell me. You've got nothing to lose; I'm just a girl on the highway. Why were you scowling at me back there when you passed me?"

"I wasn't scowling," he protested. Then after some thought, said, "I guess maybe you caught me singing."

"So you followed me all this way to make sure I don't think you're a dork?"

He started to argue, then laughed loudly. "No, nothing like that. You tell me. What is it about you that made me follow you all this way?"

"I don't know, but my winning smile and my awesome driving ability don't seem to cut the mustard here, when you have the American Dream back at the exit."

"I don't know." he said, "I've never done anything like this, but I just want to keep talking to you."

So talk, he did. I don't know if he sat at the exit or drove around his neighborhood, but for the next two hours while I continued north, 390 told me about his wife ("my best friend—you'd love her"); his children ("a father's dream"); his job ("my own business, worth a few million"); his religion ("God first, then the rest"); and only reluctantly ended our conversation when I had to stop to pee and he realized it was dinnertime at home.

"Text me when you get where you're going. I want to know you arrived safely," he said sincerely. "Where are you headed, anyway?" He asked, suddenly aware that the entire conversation had been about him.

"Just heading up north for the week," I replied.

"For a vacation? What do you do anyway?"

"Anything I want," I replied, thinking back to a line my brother used to convey that he didn't have the responsibilities of a family. But I was using it differently. I was creating a new life.

The answer intrigued my new friend, and I could almost hear him nodding his approval. "I should have known," was all he answered.

"Listen, 390, as much as I've enjoyed talking to you, I don't want to get you in trouble. Maybe we should call it a day."

"She's going out tonight," he said, practically cutting me off. "I'll be home with the kids. I'd like to continue our conversation. Please don't forget."

"Okay then, but you should know that whatever mess you get into is your own responsibility. Got it?" I surprised myself with that little bit of confidence, and I wasn't sure if I felt sneaky or excited, but I did know that I was only in it for an adventure, and the Universe dropped him here next to me, so I was going to see where it took me. *He started it* was becoming my mantra, giving me the convenient illusion that I had no responsibility for these oddly-formed, socially- and morally-unacceptable relationships.

"Fair enough. So you'll text me later?"

"We'll see. Go eat dinner with your kids."

Chapter 14

A New Theory

arrived at the cottage around 9 p.m., and after unloading the car and getting settled, I took up my phone and there was a text waiting for me from 390.

Arrive yet?

I responded: Just now. Miss me already?

390: Yes.

I was actually a little startled by the sense of urgency. Part excitement, part curiosity. *Who was this stranger in my phone?*

I gave 390 and his sudden appearance a bit of thought. After the year I'd had, and the state I was in now, on my way out of such a deep depression, the only thing I was certain of was that I needed to find a new foundation on which to build the new life I hadn't bargained for. In a year that had been full of judgment, perceived from others, and heaped on myself, I wanted to let go of it all and change course completely. I only knew that what I knew wasn't what I needed to know anymore.

I had become more curious about how other people walked through life. How did they handle their jobs, their relationships, their kids? I wanted to see what was at their core, at the base of them. I didn't know what was true for me anymore, and nothing I knew was real, so it seemed like a perfect time to investigate others and see what would be the best way to rewrite my own life. I wanted to be open to the magic of the Universe using truly raw material: honesty without judgment. I was willing to be the guinea pig for any experiment that would show me the truth, and 390 seemed to appear out of nowhere to help me.

What is it you need from me? I texted.

I don't know, but you do, don't you?

I stared at the text for a minute, trying to be honest, but nothing came to me.

Attraction, 390 answered his own question. You're like a magnet. A shiver went up my spine, wondering what I had attracted, and he asked, Are you busy, or can I call you now?

I tried to protest the call, but he was short on time, and wanted to hear my voice.

"I prefer text," I said when he dialed. "I like to see what you're thinking, and to process your words. I'm very visual," I explained.

"I'm auditory," he countered. "I spend a lot of time on the phone, and I can understand you better when I can hear your inflections."

Well, okay then. Here we go.

It became apparent that I would have to learn to be quick-witted, charming and graceful on the fly if I was going to pull off whatever new identity, or peel back whatever layer, I was working on uncovering. I decided I was up for the challenge, the adventure. Bring it on, Stranger.

"Okay, 390. What are you looking for? You said you were happily married, you love your job, your kids, and your God. So why are you sneaking out behind the shed to talk to me while your wife is out?"

"I'm not sure," he said again. "It's like I was drawn to you. What have you got to offer me?" He asked with a nervous laugh.

"I'm not offering anything," I said seriously. Then, I suppose in an effort to dare us both into moving it along, or finish this, I continued, "but I'm open to any possibilities and opportunities that may arise."

"Wow," was all he said.

After a bit of silence, and a few nervous sighs from the other end of the line, I decided to just say whatever came next. I was tired, and he was married, so I didn't have much to lose on launching into my thoughts. "I have a theory," I said.

Immediately intrigued, I could hear him settle in and relax. "What kind of theory?"

"Love, adventure, possibility, opportunity," I said before he finished. "It's why you followed me back onto the road, and it's why you need me now."

"I wouldn't say I *need* you," he said, defensively, then quickly followed it with, "I just like talking to you."

"No, you need me," I said, confidently, almost condescendingly. "And I'll tell you why, but first, let me ask you this: Who's your best friend?"

"What does that have to do with anything?"

"Do you even have a best friend?" I asked. "Do you have any friends?"

"Sure I do," he answered indignantly. "I've got my brothers, some guys from work…"

"Exactly," I said, not really sure about how to explain, but trusting that if he was meant to hear them, the words would find their way to him. "Your friends are guys you already have a defined, task-related relationship with. But do you have any-one you just hang out with? A poker group or…"

"I don't gamble," he interjected, as if it was an implied sermon.

I ignored his holy admonishment. "What I mean is, do you make any effort, like your wife is tonight, to meet with people that aren't part of your already-defined, neatly-woven life?" I hated to mention his wife but it was the only illustra-tion I could think of.

"I have a few friends, but I don't see them very often because we all work a lot, and I'd really rather spend my free time with my family."

"Yes, of course. Men like you, with goals and plans and priorities, tend to focus on one vision. You spend all your time working toward realizing that vision, every day, for the benefit of your growing family, am I right?"

"Yes, that's exactly right. I work hard so I can enjoy my life with them."

"And that makes you feel noble and worthy of all your accomplishments, yes?"

He snorted, probably in embarrassment, so I continued. "But wasn't there a movie about a guy who went crazy because he was all work and no play?"

"Jack Nicholson. *The Shining*. The book was better, but what a classic character," he confirmed, wandering off the point.

"And a perfect illustration of what happens when you give up your own time and dreams so you can work for everyone else's. You went crazy, but instead of taking an ax through the house, you picked up a girl on the interstate."

390 laughed. It was a tentative, uncomfortable laugh, yet it still made me smile. It wasn't going to take me much longer to make the point; he knew where I was going.

"So you're saying it's either get drunk with friends or have an affair? Sounds like you're trying to make this a mid-life crisis, and…"

"Not exactly; I think it's more than that. You are drawn to me because, if my theory is correct, you need an adventurous outlet to try on that part of you that isn't your pillar of strength: your dreams. Dreams are fragile, and you cannot always trust them to the people you already have in your life, who expect certain things of you, based on your common commitments. So you need me to show you the possibilities that you can't see, because you're too busy working on your set goals that are in front of you.

"Look," I continued, "everyone has categories of people in their lives: parents, children, friends, co-workers. Each of these groups fulfills a specific need in your life—to be nurtured, to play, to achieve goals. If you look at these categories, there are always more than one person in a category. *Except the spouse.* A spouse is expected to fulfill partnership, sexual, visionary, parental, and financial dreams and goals, all in one. How can one person do all that? Especially without other outlets to feed the soul?"

"I'm not sure I understand," he said thoughtfully. "My wife is awesome."

"I think you were drawn to me because you could tell, whether it was by the way I drive or smile or wave, that I am the person that you would trust with the stuff you're not ready to bring home."

"That's crazy. My wife and I share everything; she's everything to me."

"Okay then, I'm wrong. It was nice talking to you, 390." I had fully intended to hang up, but I knew he wasn't going to let me.

"Wait, wait, wait," he said. "Don't hang up. Just because I like talking to you doesn't mean I've given up on my wife."

"Of course not; I never said that. She is your life partner, the love of your life. I believed you each of the several times you've told me today," I said, not entirely facetiously. "But suppose you have a dream you're not sure goes along with the Master Plan? Suppose you need some time to think it through, someone to bounce it off, to see if it really qualifies as a dream before you upset the family dynamic with a curve ball?"

"So since I have no friends to confide in, you think I sought you out?"

"It's only a theory; but right now, I represent a new possibility and opportunity. I think you saw that, and I think maybe you need a little something to spark a fire in you, that's all. Maybe it'll just be this conversation. Maybe we'll meet secretly for sex in a Starbucks' bathroom; maybe we'll check in once a year with a list of dreams to account for. Who knows? But you need some kind of outlet, and you found it today in the car."

There was a long silence, and then a heavy sigh on the other end of the line.

"I have to go. Her car is pulling in."

"Goodnight, 390." My heart dropped a little bit. I had just engaged him, and it was over before it began.

A minute later, my phone buzzed with a text: I think you're right. Call you tomorrow?

Text first, I replied with a winky-face, and drifted happily to sleep, with absolute certainty that I was about to embark on a new adventure.

Chapter 15

The Great Debate

The text came at 7:15 a.m.: Good morning. I'm at the office, and I need to get some things taken care of. Can I call you around 8? I'll be on the road by then.

I wasn't crazy about this, but I also didn't want my new, intriguing friend to try to text while he was driving that behemoth of a truck, so I texted back, I guess that means I have to get in the shower now.

Don't put that thought in my head. I'll call you in a bit.

At 7:45, he updated, I'll be here for a few more minutes. What are you wearing?

Nothing yet, but probably jeans and boots.

Sounds hot either way.

I giggled to myself. *What does this guy want?*

390 knew something I did not, but I was ready to find out. He found me, followed me, initiated the texts, and always had the last word. In the society we live in, it's usually called *stalking;* but I knew it, *felt it,* as something more. Not change-my-life more; I was just having fun with my new sense of Girl Power, mistaken often, as I had recently, for how many men I could catch in the net. My inner yearning for honesty, truth, and love were still fighting for space with my outer desire to be desired, so I let my ego enjoy its walk in the park, something it needed to do, and I knew it would come in time, so *Trust*

became my *modus operandi*. 390 was curiously invested in me and thought I was some kind of magical sorceress that could make things happen, and he wanted to believe it was so. And I wanted to believe it was so.

And so that is what I would become.

I relished this new identity, and I became assertive and confidently told him everything I thought about anything, including a daily revisiting of my "theory" against his inability to come up with an answer for why a faithful man would be texting a girl he followed up the interstate.

He was not used to a woman being in charge; he was devoted to his God, who was clearly a man, yet he quite liked that I didn't cow to that. I found that I loved challenging—and being challenged by—390, and many discussions began with an accepted premise, to be dissected in detailed text, and one of us would wind up on the other side by the end of it.

Any topic—religion, philosophy, marital and, heaven forbid, *pre*-marital relations—were allowed; nothing was off limits. We talked, we texted, we argued, we discussed, and we changed each other's opinions. It was all so stimulating with 390.

As a little girl, I argued so much that my mother had always hoped I'd become a lawyer; but with 390, I discovered my arguments had more relevance than merely strategy over statutes. My heart was affecting his thoughts, or maybe the other way around, but I felt like someone was listening to me, which had such value to me, because within my marriage, X had always questioned my authority on everything. If it wasn't backed up by two credible sources, one of which had to be either CNN or his mother, my thoughts were worthless to him. But with 390, I felt like our minds were expanding, becoming more flexible to see everything in a new light.

Even when he didn't like the place we were going with a particular topic, 390 was always respectful of my opinion, and dare I say there were times I even changed his mind. Conversely, I relished the days when a hard-fought duel was behind us, and I found myself in defeat, accepting of a new idea that stood the test of our rigorous argument. I'd never known anyone that I thought was so mistaken in certain beliefs, yet so convicted in them. 390 won my respect so easily for his willingness to defend those convictions, as well as to allow a harlot such as myself to believe otherwise, and engage in serious debate nevertheless. I loved this guy.

But then, 390 wanted to meet.

In truth, there was never any intention on my part to infringe on the family to which he was clearly devoted. I'd had the luxury of my marriage falling apart on its own, organically. I would have been devastated if outside forces such as another woman had sabotaged it; but that wasn't my game. 390 and I had an easy rapport; we talked without shame about every-thing, as if we were research partners in a lab. Our curiosity was academic. I respected his family from the moment he told me about them. I told him often that what happened between us, was between us; but that what happened between he and his wife was none of my business. Whether it was my cheap attempt at a disclaimer or not, I didn't want him getting too wrapped up or coming to expect too much from me. I'd just finally felt the freedom of letting go of a relationship, so why would I want to do that again—and with someone who was unavailable? Yet, neither of us could put a finger on the exact reason he remained reluctant to tell his wife that he'd made a new friend. And I could not deny that I was attracted to this new stranger. My desire clouded my intention as the exhilaration of our theoretical arguments gained momentum.

So a couple of weeks into it, 390 texted that he was heading to an appointment in my neck of the woods; or more accurately, what I told him was my neck of the woods, and would I like to meet?

You mean for coffee? I don't drink coffee.

Maybe something else? He fished.

The Starbucks' bathroom? I teased, I'll bet we could do some damage in there. ;)

It was a silly attempt at sexting, since I had told myself that this was just another funny story about a guy in a car; but once 390 got hold of the image of a crisp white blouse over thigh-high boots while waiting for scones and a latte, his code word for sex became "Starbucks," which, if you key-worded our text log, came up quite a bit after that. I thought it was curious, too, since he never stopped talking about how much sex he had with his beautiful wife, even with the four perfect children and their wonderful friends and their perfect home.

And, I thought, *therein lies the problem.*

Chapter 16

Meeting of the Minds

t was a Wednesday when I called him out.

Meet me at Starbucks on Route 90, I instructed.

You mean Route 80?

Whatever. Meet me there at 10:30, the one by the movie theater.

I arrived at the shopping mall in a t-shirt, jeans, and boots, hoping to finally get in a little trouble with my cerebral friend near the Pier 1 loading dock. They say the brain is the most sensitive sexual organ, and all the mental sparring of the last few weeks had gotten me worked up. He was the one who started it, after all.

He pulled up next to my car, and I got out and walked purposefully toward his truck. Meeting his eyes without a word, I waved him back and opened the back door of the king cab. As he got out to follow my lead, I slammed the door.

"A car seat? Are you serious?" I yelled in frustration.

"I had to take my son to preschool this morning!"

I walked around to the other side, and he followed. As he made his way toward me, I began picking gummy dinosaurs and Cheerios off the seat.

"I've got a better idea," I said. "Let's take a walk."

We found a small set of bleachers standing on the edge of a swampy expanse. What they were used for was anyone's guess, but it was good enough for us. I held out my hand for him to hold, and he wound his fingers through mine. *There.* We sat for an uncomfortable amount of time, wondering silently what would come next. He thought he had come to kiss me, and I thought I had come as a vixen. Sitting there with him though, I decided that I liked his heart too much to ruin our connection with a cheap thrill. Instinctively, I unwound my hand, and hooked my arm through his, lightly, easily.

"How about you tell me what's what?" I ventured.

"What do you mean?"

"Listen, 390, I'm not here to mess with your head. I know you're very happily married and you love your family. I like you, but not enough to make you hate yourself, so why don't you just tell me what's on your mind *right now*. Just say what's true."

"How do you know I want to say anything?"

"Because you wouldn't be here if you didn't want to tell me something."

"How do you know this?" He paused, and then added incredulously, "It's like you...*know.*"

"Yep, I'm magic, never forget that," I said with a sigh that exhaled the seduction out of the equation. "Now here's what I'm going to say that's true: you can tell me anything. I mean *anything.* And you don't have to be afraid of it, or me, because we don't really exist. I'm like your invisible friend. Nobody knows we're here, so nobody has to know what we talk about."

This had quickly become more than a conquest for me. This was a meeting of the minds; a true love match, and it didn't require anything except a willingness to participate honestly in whatever was about to unfold. All I wanted was to know what was real. Ironic, since I had been making everything up as I went along, but the façade of life's details didn't matter. This guy had an unexpressed heart, full of something that was important to him, and he was reaching out to me, trusting me.

"You mean..." he stammered, "you mean you're okay if we just talk?"

I giggled. "Of course," I said, "I may be worth more to you as a friend than as the girl you think you met racing along 390."

"380."

"Whatever. Let it go, already. Tell me what you want to say."

He pressed his lips together and shook his head from side to side, as if it pained him to have someone in his head.

"Nobody's ever asked me..."

"Well, I want to know. What is important to you? *Right now.*"

He squeezed his eyes together with his thumb and forefinger, wincing, and then looking up, he cleared his throat. "I have this idea. It's big," he said, barely audible. I leaned in as he continued, "I've never put it into words, it's just been swirling around in my head. But I'm working to really secure my business so that I can turn it into something. I want to start a foundation. I can't really hash it out because I don't want to deviate from the business plan I already have in place. It works, and everybody's happy with the way it's all going, so I can't just change the game plan without really thinking it through, but I don't know where to start."

Was there an echo? It seemed that my theory had been right on target! It was a real moment for me, too, to acknowledge that following the path to 390 led not only to a purposeful connection, but a confirmation of my instincts.

We talked for over an hour about his business, working his ideas into words and then into projects. It was such a rush for me, because I knew nothing about business, but I followed the trail, asking questions that he needed to hear out loud, so he could talk them through and clarify his thoughts. I found out that I loved to learn new things, even things I had no use for, such as the particular business in which 390 had invested his life.

I jumped off the bleacher and turned to him. He hesitated, so I stepped back and took his hands in mine. I spread his arms out as far as mine would expand, and quickly dropped my arms and hugged him around his middle, leaning my cheek into his chest. I lifted my head and gave him a soft kiss on the cheek, nothing remotely resembling the premise set forth earlier in the day. "I'm glad we met. Now go home."

I turned to go, and he grabbed my hand for an instant before he let it fall, and I walked to my car, got in and drove away. I pulled around the rows of delivery bays and stopped to pull out my phone. I'm here if you need me—Your invisible friend.

Later that evening, he texted me from the exit ramp. Thanks for listening. I appreciate that more than what we met for. Is that weird?

Not at all. Glad we got that out of the way. :)

I still think you're hot.

You'll never know, I replied with a winky face, and went back to making dinner.

Over the course of the next few weeks, 390 texted me almost every day while he was at work. Once we became clear that he wasn't out to have an affair, that we were both safe, I became completely fearless in talking about sex with him. For the sake of exploration in a safe environment, something neither of us had in strict religious upbringings, anything was on the table for me. For him, he had a fantasy in place that would never call him out of his comfort zone. He knew I would never let him cheat on his wife, so I could be anything to him, and he and I could talk a big game, but never have to prove it.

Every once in a while, he would ask to call me, and he would tease out a hairy business issue, and then return to sex talk. I was the elusive best friend he could never name. I had no idea that I could have charged him for business consulting; but I kept telling myself to remind him that he should at least put me on the board of his foundation. There were so many things I loved about 390, but I was especially fond of his ability to push me out of my comfort zone and test my limits. There had been little things, like figuring out in the space of a text message where to find the perfect place in "my neighborhood" to send him for lunch and give a review as if I'd been there a million times; but then there were bigger things, like pretending the sex shop was my second home, when in fact I had never been to one in my entire life before I dared to go for the benefit of the illusion. He would text while I browsed around, looking at vibrators and fishnet stockings, and I would ask him what kind of condoms he used, and he would, of course, say that he was faithfully married and never used one. When I stood at the counter, meeting the eyes of the clerk as he handed me a plain brown bag full of naughty treats I'd never before had the nerve to buy, I felt so powerful, and 390 was awestruck by my confidence. To seal the dare, I would call him from the parking lot, as I watched men with sunglasses and baseball caps go into the store after having parked as far from the entrance as possible, ashamed of their own physical needs, whatever they might be. But 390, through his fears, gave me the courage—if only perceived—to pull my minivan into the first spot and act like it was a regular stop on the way to drop off the dry cleaning. By acting the part for 390, I had discovered a courage I never knew I had.

As the summer approached, I told 390 that I would be going away for a week. I had to have oral surgery, and I wasn't sure I'd be able to talk. I was a big baby when it came to toothaches, so I'd anticipated being incoherent on painkillers for at least that long. He suggested that this might be a good place to leave it, and although we both felt sad, I had to agree that it felt like the right thing to do. It was a bittersweet goodbye, and I went for a long walk after he signed off for the last time, shocked into a grief that confused me.

I was confused by my "adventure" pulling me in too deep. I had fooled us both into a lighthearted, magical, carefree existence, and I hadn't realized until then that he was more than just a textual diversion from my responsibility-laden days. I had loved this man, in the truest version of the word. We hadn't shared our lives, but however briefly, we had shared our souls. I walked until I had cried, laughed at myself for crying over what I had created, and then I really felt the love and gratitude for this man who had given me the gift of allowing me to see truths in myself I hadn't before. He had been my flagship of love, adventure, possibility and opportunity, all rolled into one. As I reflected on this, I vowed to make those four words my daily prayer, for I had never felt so alive and meaningful and *present* as I had with him.

Chapter 17

Spring Cleaning

The summer solstice was fast approaching, and after a ridiculously active spring, I was lonely once again. Turnpike Steve had finally faded away, and 390 had helped me to ease his disappearance, only to disappear himself. Even my massage therapist had "fired" me, citing an unethical physical attraction—which I thought was hilarious and flattering, but nevertheless left me with yet another lonely rejection.

I had my surgery, and bless him, the dentist gave me several prescriptions to last me as long as I could possibly claim to have pain. I mostly took the ones that made me loopy, so I wouldn't check my phone for the texts that had stopped coming.

In the days that followed, I was busy with the kids and all their year-end activities, school field trips, field days, preschool ceremonies, and one last playdate for everyone before we parted for the summer.

I had almost a month to pack for our summer at the cottage, as X decided that he would like to have the kids on Independence Day weekend. Since he lived in a city that exploded with fireworks and celebration, I thought that was more than fair; but the hurry-up days of school ending, followed by the waiting of summer to begin at the cottage was more than I could bear.

With no extra-textular activities to keep me occupied, I was forced to turn my attention to the task of packing up X's stuff. Since I had made the request that he not come too deep into the house when the kids were around, and since the kids were always around, I—offered? agreed? was coerced?—to box up and clear out all the stuff he'd left behind.

This was a painful process that I had started and stopped so many times in the past, but I couldn't put it off any longer; he'd been gone for months and he wasn't coming back. In his office, which would become the guest room if I could just get through this exercise, there were photos, ticket stubs, awards, newspaper and magazine articles, and all manner of memories that flooded my heart with the fairy tale of what had been, and the agonizing mind-fuck of what might have been.

Grandma Sitter had instinctively understood my grief, so when I refused her offer to help sort through X's space, she created daily excursions on which to take the kids, even though she had planned on the summer off while we were away.

I threw away what I could; I boxed up things for the kids to look at when we die. But there were so many questions about some of the things in that room that I just didn't know what to do with them. I called X and asked him what he thought I should do with priceless, framed keepsakes that he had received throughout his career. "Just throw them away," he said dismally, "I don't have enough room in my apartment, and I don't have time to get a storage space and transport it. Just throw it all out." It was clear he didn't have any idea what to do, either, and he didn't want to think about it.

X was miserable. I hated that we had to have the discussion, but we had put everything pertaining to our impending divorce on hold so we could deal with the kids. There had been no rush; we were finished being married, but neither of us were anxious to do it again, and financially speaking, we weren't in a hurry to divide the assets. We didn't hate each other; we just hated being married to each other. Still, the slow-paced deconstruction was torture.

I waded through most of it, just looking at all the stuff he'd accumulated over the years. How could I organize it all? Some of it would certainly have to be thrown out, but so much of it was important to the career X had built, and the person he had become. Absent husband and depressed dad aside, he was a good man, and it wasn't fair to just expunge the record of his achievements. Personally, I wanted to clear out everything in this room for my own sanity; yet I couldn't bring myself to eliminate the tangible memories of his accomplishments, things that someday his children would appreciate and be proud of. I cursed him for being so hard to hate. I wanted to despise him, but I looked around the room, and became conscious of the fact that he had provided all of it for me. I could do what I wanted with it; he had stopped caring about his legacy. But this stuff, this room, this house…he had worked hard for all of it, to give to us.

I sat on the floor and cried until I couldn't see straight, and then I drove to the shipping store for boxes and packed it all, not neatly, just accounted for, into the attic for another day, perhaps one day when we could purposefully decide what to do with the possessions that had once been so important to us.

Chapter 18

Independence Day

Occasionally, I exchanged a text or two with Wendy from Cancún; a forgotten photo here, a funny memory there. As summer began, she sent me a text saying that Jeff's brother and his wife had split up, and asked if it would be too much to text him to offer my support?

I liked the brother. He'd had a wicked sense of humor, and we'd had a few laughs during our very brief acquaintance. Maybe the Universe was sending me another shot at possibility, but I was kind of getting tired of already used, married guys. Still, my text log was pretty sparse as of late, and I wanted to have another adventure; and since I didn't connect with his wife at all, that could have been the reason I agreed. Sure, I texted, I'll lift his spirits!

For the next week, the poor guy texted me every day after work, admittedly drunk and distraught over his wife's having left him, ironically, for a text lover. Having just closed my own attic door, I couldn't have been happier to give him something to do besides pack up her stuff for whenever she might want to get it, which would probably be never. He was completely heartbroken and embarrassed and vulnerable, and it dawned on me that I was the only one he could lean on—a stranger. So after about a week, when he suggested for the thirtieth time that we should get together, I replied, Pick a place, I'll meet you.

What the hell, summer had begun, and I was ready for a fling. He lived in Wisconsin, so he picked Minneapolis for the big rendezvous destination, and by the next day, he had picked out flights and a hotel, and called Jeff and Wendy to arrange for them to come, too, so it wouldn't be too awkward. For him, anyway.

But, whatever, I was all about adventure, so I took a deep breath—*here we go*.

I booked a flight, and there was no looking back until our Cancún reunion in two weeks. I was actually pretty excited. The whole thing sounded just crazy and unexpected enough to be fun.

Except for when he sent me the inevitable endless text comprised of about seven concurrent bubbles that vomited onto my screen on the Fourth of July, saying he just couldn't do it. He was distraught, and not thinking, and he was sorry to lead me on, but his pain needed to be worked through, and, and, and…

Somehow I should have known all that drunk texting wouldn't end well.

Upon my notification of this awkward development, Jeff answered my text to Wendy, and said that his brother's behavior was so uncharacteristically pathetic that we should find his wife and beat her to a pulp for what she'd reduced him to, and…that was the last I ever heard from any of them.

Getting dumped after two weeks of drunken texts, over a holiday weekend no less, was a little painful. X had the kids for the traditional barbeque-and-fireworks celebration, and I was alone, tagging along to a country club carnival with friends. Needless to say, it wasn't much of a celebration. I mean, I was glad the country had survived another year and all, but my ego was pretty beat up. This guy and I had hit it off months ago. He had seen me in a bathing suit, and I had put myself out there for him. Then this drunken home-improvement sad-sack of a sales guy gets to reject me?

But that was the part where they say it's just an opportunity wrapped up as a bummer, or something like that, and since I was newly minted in the *There's A Reason For Everything* club, I chose to take the high road to see where it led. I was stuck with a non-refundable plane ticket, and hell if I was not going to find me some adventure in Minneapolis, *goddammit*. I switched hotels, upgraded myself to one with a spa, and treated myself to a cute pair of shoes and some adorable undergarments, anyway, because I was going to find someone to appreciate them. In Minneapolis. I could hardly think it without laughing out loud.

Chapter 19

Girlfriend's Weekend

The day I left for what I referred to as "Girlfriend's Weekend," should anyone have asked, there were great storms across the Midwest. Flights were cancelled, delayed, and diverted, and I was beginning to doubt that the trip was a very wise choice on my part. My flight took me through Detroit, where for reasons unknown to me, I was upgraded to first class for the flight into Minneapolis-St. Paul. I boarded the plane that Friday afternoon, took my aisle seat in the front row, and texted the only person who knew where I was: I am surrounded by a bunch of boring businessmen.

Irritated and uncomfortable with the collection of stuffed shirts, I looked at my phone, where Kali had sent a reply: Opportunity!

I put a smile on my face and said hello to each of them: an older, overweight but jovial water treatment salesman who sat next to me, and two colleagues across the aisle that periodically leered at me as they compared notes on their morning meeting.

The flight was delayed because of weather. The man across the aisle from me began to squirm. And again the flight was delayed for mechanical difficulties. And the man began to get agitated. And finally, an announcement was made that should we care to deplane, another announcement would be made when the plane was ready to go. The thought never occurred to me to get off the plane and just go home; I was determined to prove to myself that a whiny weasel from Wisconsin couldn't break my spirit of adventure.

The squirmy man turned to me and said, "We're going to the Admiral's Club for a drink. Would you care to join us?"

I'm not sure why I said no; maybe because he was not attractive, maybe it was his squirmy nature, maybe because I had passed a little place by the food court where I could get a better snack. Or maybe, my common sense regarding unattractive squirmy strangers kicked in. In any case, I declined the invitation. "Thanks, anyway," I smiled brightly, "I'll see you when you get back."

He handed me his business card and asked, "If you get back before us, will you call me when the plane is fixed?"

"Sure, I'll text you," I replied, my common sense scurrying away, along with him and his colleagues.

Two hours later, with a new gate assignment and a shiny new plane, we all settled once and for all into our seats. My seatmate was anxiously emailing his office about connecting flights, so that left…the squirmy guy. He tried repeatedly to strike up a conversation with me, even as it was obvious that I was trying to read my book, but one thing I had learned by that point as a parent was that when a kid wants your attention, it's a lot easier to give it to him from the start, rather than be worn down later on. I closed my book, and was surprised to find that I really enjoyed talking to him. He was quite an adventure-seeker, Squirmy was, and he used every last mileage point he had from his extensive business travel to make his vacations count. He had been to the North Pole, the South

Pole, the Equator, and everywhere along the way. But that didn't make him suddenly attractive; nor did the point when he mentioned he had a Harley and would be happy to give me a motorcycle tour of Minneapolis the next morning. But it did pass the time nicely.

"That's a generous offer, thank you," I said, wincing at the memory of a ride from a friend in college that had ended with third-degree-burned flesh as a result of my leg hitting the exhaust pipe. "If my girlfriends are okay with it, I'll give you a call." This girlfriend story was beginning to roll off the tongue. By the time the flight was on its final descent, I had three girlfriends, all named with full bios, and histories of our friendships.

I said goodbye to my seatmate, thanked the squirmy guy again for his offer, and headed to the public transportation system so I could save a few bucks and not have to talk to a cab driver for an hour. I had wasted a third of my getaway weekend by then, and I just wanted my adventure to begin.

I rode through the suburbs, past the stadiums, and into the city, and finally got off the train and began the six-block walk to my swanky hotel in the sweltering, record-setting heat. Halfway there, the skies opened up and a thunderous joke began to rain down on me and my adorable new sundress.

Seriously.

What the fuck am I doing here?

As I waited at the hotel desk for my room key, I bravely texted Kali to tell her that I had no idea why I came here, but I was certain the answer would come, and I wasn't going to worry about it. Adventure. That's what I'm here for. And I closed my eyes and said a prayer to make it so.

But as I made my way to the elevator, a cold, hollow feeling took over and I suddenly felt alone, not adventurous at all. I was lost. I was lost in Minneapolis, lonely in a way I hadn't felt since X moved out. A hopeless, lonesome lost in a strange city. To hell with the Wisconsin Weasel; I wanted to get on the next flight home and go back to where it was safe. Who was I fooling into thinking I'd just go somewhere and meet someone for an adventure? Only myself. The pain of loss enveloped me again, and I put my sunglasses on in the elevator and cried silently all the way to the 18th floor and down the hall to my room.

Chapter 20

The Perv

With no idea what to do next, but not wanting to spend the weekend crying and lonely, I thought anything was better than nothing. Nothing totally sucks, so I texted Jeff's brother, the Wisconsin Weasel: I'm in MSP! If you're up for it, come meet me for a drink. I don't bite.

Another lesson I learned quickly was to never say you don't bite in a text. It never comes off right.

I went for my pre-booked massage and with no response from my text upon my return, the heat outside sending wavy air like a desert movie up to my window, and nothing but the room service menu looking at me, I crawled into bed, hoping to finish a good cry and maybe get it out of my system and go home.

Then Kali's text came: You're not there to sleep. Go find your adventure.

Dammit.

She was right, of course. If I was going to be stuck there, miserable, something was better than nothing. The rain had stopped so I got dressed and, fighting my resistance, took the elevator down to the lobby. I asked the concierge to send me somewhere, anywhere, where there might be people. She pointed me out the door of the hotel, and after a few blocks, I found myself at a Minnesota Twins baseball game. I wasn't a big baseball fan, but I could appreciate a night at the stadium, so I bought a cheap ticket and worked my way up to the "nosebleed" seats, against a backdrop of one of the most beautiful sunsets I'd ever seen, thinking that it might be a sign that I'd find some gorgeous Midwesterner to keep me company. I scanned the crowd, hoping there would be someone to compliment the scenery; but there wasn't a single face up there worth a text.

I wasn't hungry, I didn't drink, and I didn't care who was at bat, so I left my seat and began to roam around the stadium. If nothing else, I'd check out the gift shop and bring something back for the kids. When would they ever get to see an official Minnesota Twins anything? Never, because I wasn't planning on doing this again, ever. I bought a couple of baseballs and some bat-shaped pens, and made my way, still alone, toward the exit. *Enough with this!* I was flat-out sad. And annoyed. And lonely. And at a loss as to why the hell I was still there. And even as I laughed that sardonic, pitiful, self-punishing laugh, all I wanted was to go back to the hotel and cry myself to sleep.

But I wasn't even at the exit gate yet. Trying to keep my mascara from streaking in the heat and the tears that were forthcoming at bay, I wiped my eyes as the crowd suddenly burst into applause and chants and howls and whatever else crowds do as the home team ties up the game in the bottom of the ninth. I was suddenly in a sea of revelers, practically carrying me to the exit; at one point, a happy, drunk fellow picked me up and tried to put me on his shoulders in celebration. I thought that the fire marshals of Minnesota might want to check on the exit policy for the stadium, because with no say in the matter, the super-condensed crowd had carried me into the bar just outside the stadium gates before my feet were on the ground again. It was both frightening and endearing that people got this worked up over their sports addictions, and I found myself at the bar for extra innings, surrounded by a small group of men a few years older than myself, all looking at me with the same once-over, as I was sure I was giving each of them.

"I'm a porno producer," announced the shortest one, predictably. "I'd love for you to be the star of my next blockbuster."

Are you fucking kidding me, Universe? This is all you got for me?

The other guys rolled their eyes, but I wasn't going to take that shit anymore.

"You're kidding!" I shrieked excitedly, leaning in as close as I could without actually touching him. "I just finished filming one last week! Do you have a card?"

This made the short fellow nervous—but uncontrollably and visibly excited south of his border, and his friends exploded in laughter. They asked what I was drinking, and in my frustration with the Universe, the tequila began to flow.

There were three of them besides Porno Pete, all out for a Guy's Night reunion. I learned that two of them were married, and all I could make of the last one was that he was a grumpy drunk, who leered at me and grabbed my ass.

"You'll have to pay for that," I said as I smacked him.

"How much you want? You got a great body," he slurred.

"You don't have enough," I said, "not in your home equity, not in your kids' college funds, not in your mid-life crisis car. So hands off."

He straightened up and began talking about his kids. "I have three boys," he said. Then he looked me up and down, and focused his gaze on my chest, and declared, "you seem like you'd be a good mom."

"I'm a great mom," I said, squatting down to meet his eyes and forcing them back up to my face. "I have the most awesome kids in the world," and he thought that gave him permission to grab my ass again. So I smacked him again.

The grumpy little troll, all indignant, took a while to steady himself upright, but finally announced that he was leaving. Completely unaffected by this turn of events, his friends and I continued to have a few more shots, which lifted my mood somewhat, but I certainly wasn't seeing the adventure in these guys before they saw me back to my hotel four blocks away. I texted Kali their pictures so she'd know who to put on the *Wanted* poster if I turned up missing, and told the bartender to study their faces as we left, and keep an eye on the news later, just in case.

They dropped me off, and the tall one said, "Hey, would you mind calling Grumpy? I think you hurt his feelings, and he won't answer our calls."

"Sure," I said. "I've had six tequila shots, but for Grumpy, anything." I blew the guys a kiss after the tall one entered the number into my phone, and walked surprisingly gingerly to the elevator.

When I got back to my room, I texted Kali to let her know I was alone and safe, and then I completed the call to Grumpy.

"What makes you think you know me?" He began, in what memory serves as a drunken high-school-era rant.

"I don't need to know you. Just checking in to see if you're safe," I answered.

"You really do care about me. I knew it. My wife doesn't have sex with me."

"Um. Okay then. Thanks for sharing that."

"Well sure," he slurred some more, "just because I'm a pervert and I'm the only one willing to admit it."

"Okay, well, pervs are people, too. I don't hold it against you. Goodnight."

Seriously, Universe. I've had it. What's with all the completely unacceptable married men?

I brushed my teeth and marveled at how I was still standing after all that alcohol, since I was normally a lightweight and didn't drink because I usually lost consciousness after one beer. I curled up on the bed and looked out onto the city of Minneapolis and hoped that I hadn't used up all my adventure points, and promptly passed out.

Chapter 21

Lady of the Lake

The next morning, there was a text from a number I didn't recognize, and a voicemail. I checked the voicemail first: "Hello, this is *mdakfjarth* and it's a beautiful day for a ride. It's going to get very hot out later, so I'd like to meet you before I leave for my lake house for the rest of the weekend."

Ride? Did I meet someone?...oh! It's the squirmy guy from the plane. What was his name? I fumbled around for the business card I'd shoved in my bag yesterday. Eventually, I gave up looking. I didn't really care, anyway. *Mdakfjarth, Squirmy, what's the difference? He's just another one of the Universe's bad jokes.* My head hurt, but in some sudden burst of stranger etiquette, I didn't want him to think me rude, so I called him back immediately.

"I'm so sorry; I went out last night and had a little too much to drink," I said, as if I owed him an explanation.

"Oh well, I'm not leaving for a couple of hours yet, and there's so much you should see. Call me in an hour and see how you feel then."

"Sure, I'll go sit in the steam room and see if it helps. Call you in an hour."

I hung up and checked the text: Good morning. Thank you for checking on me last night. I'm sorry if I acted like an ass.

Well geez, that narrows it down. The bar was full of people acting like an ass. Did I give my number out? I texted back a generic: I'm glad you're okay.

It wasn't two seconds before the reply: My wife doesn't like sex.

Ah. Now I remember.

I fell back asleep and an hour later, the phone woke me up. It was the squirmy guy asking if I felt any better.

"You'd better go without me. I really hate to turn down your offer, but I'd hate even more to throw up on your Harley. Have a great weekend."

I went back to sleep for the third time when Kali texted: How's the adventure going?

Crap. It was officially time to get up, severe dehydration and hangover notwithstanding: I'm going, I'm going.

I put on jeans, a t-shirt, and flip-flops, the only clothes I had that weren't silk or lace or spike heels, cursed myself for not having had a reason for wearing the others yet, and headed out of the hotel.

Minneapolis, and I'd been told, a number of other outdoorsy-type cities, had this great citywide biking system I'd never seen before, where you could rent a bicycle on any corner and leave it on any other corner. *Genius*. I thought this might be a nice way to get around faster than walking in the heat, and to get some air moving so I wouldn't throw up, so I studied the kiosk for a good bit of time, trying to figure out how it worked, and after a while, my eyes were able to focus and I slid my credit card in the slot and took out a bike.

I had a feeling that Squirmy was going to call and check up on me, and why I cared I'll never know, but it was a good place to start, so I recalled the only thing I could remember him saying about Minneapolis, which was that it had a nice lake. In fact, Minnesota is the State of 10,000 Lakes. Yes indeed, that's even the state motto! Several of them were in the Minneapolis area, so I set my goal to bike to the nearest one.

I discovered in short order that I wasn't a cyclist. I didn't do hills, and bike lanes—c'mon, weren't they just open targets for speeding cars? But I pressed on. The lake was probably only about four or five miles from where I checked out the bicycle, but by the time I realized I was holding the map the wrong way and reading the legend incorrectly, I figured out my shortcuts were doing me no favors, and it was really more like ten.

It was 105 degrees, and I was somewhere between my air-conditioned, spa-pampering hotel and a lake, wearing jeans and designer flip-flops with fluffy pompons that kept getting caught in the pedals. I was already pretty sweaty when a very nice, college-aged cutie rode up alongside me.

"You look lost. Do you need help?"

"What gave me away?"

"Oh, let's not go there. My name is Kurt," he said, and held out a hand.

"I have a very nice car where I come from," I said sheepishly, and tried to pretend my hand wasn't too clammy.

Kurt was kind. "I'm headed down Hennepin Avenue, if that's where you're going," he offered.

"I'm headed down Hennepin, if that's the way to the lake," I hoped out loud.

"Visiting, are you?" He smirked. "There are several lakes that begin with a ride down Hennepin," he explained. "Lake Calhoun is the closest."

"Yes!" I shouted a little too eagerly. "I was told I simply must see it before I leave tomorrow."

"Alrighty, then, follow me, m'lady," he said with a grand flourish.

I thought this might be my adventure, so I dug into my pocket and produced a wand of lip gloss, the only thing I needed to prepare myself for what would surely end in a picturesque picnic with my new friend, Kurt, along the shores of Lake Calhoun.

I didn't count on the dehydration thing.

It took about four blocks for me to beg Kurt to just give me the directions and leave me to my death by this two-wheeled demon I was riding. Cute as he was, I didn't want him to witness it, nor feel responsible for saving me when it was time for me to expire.

"You sure?" he asked. "It's not much further."

"Please. Go." I panted, not so much like an overdramatic thespian, as an embarrassed, sweaty, heaving bike virgin. Mercifully, Kurt made up something about this being the turnoff for his parents' house, anyway. He pointed and instructed me to go three more blocks and turn right, and I wouldn't be able to miss Lake Calhoun, then he pedaled away.

I composed myself as I watched him go, and forced myself back on the bike. Twenty minutes later, sweating and even more dehydrated, I arrived at my destination with a sense of victory usually reserved for Olympians. I managed a surge of energy and rode along the path around the lake for a short time before I spotted a snack bar, and pulled over to drink in the joys of water and happy people splashing about in the lake.

I finished my water, and considered the bike and the impending ride home. I realized it would be getting late soon, and I'd better figure out where to dump this thing and get a bus back to town. It turned out to be easier than I thought, as the bus depot was just across from the bike drop-off at the liquor store parking lot. And the bus driver even let me ride for free, probably because I looked like I was on the last ride of my life.

Chapter 22

The Chicken Police

started back to the hotel from the bus stop when a little voice inside my head sounding very much like the next text from Kali made me turn off onto Nicolette Mall, a pedestrian plaza in downtown Minneapolis, lined with pubs and restaurants that were filled with revelers enjoying the warm Saturday night. I thought to myself, *If I can't find someone to talk to in this crowd, I'm going to see if there's a standby flight home later.*

I tried. I really tried to find a place at a communal outdoor table, to look casual and blend in with the crowd, to insert myself into a cool group. But it was just too hot. My jeans were soaked, my Lululemon t-shirt was sticking to me, my hair was matted to my scalp. I needed air conditioning. The thoughts jumbled around in my head: *I can always text the Grumpy Perv later if I'm that bored.* And: *Damn that Wisconsin Weasel.* Even: *No matter what, I'm not letting Kali text me into staying!*

I made my way into the air-blasted corner restaurant and found an open seat at the bar. As the bartender placed a desperately-needed club soda in front of me, I ordered a grilled chicken dinner.

"I wouldn't do that," a voice said, above the background chatter but clearly to me. I looked up, and a handsome man with dark eyes and a beard was settling onto the stool next to me. His group of friends all smiled at me, but took a few steps away to let their friend attack his prey, as if he was headed to prison later.

"Really? Why, was there a salmonella outbreak?" I asked, not taking the straw from the cool, bubbly water out of my mouth.

"No, but I guarantee you'll like the fried chicken better. It's a specialty."

"How can you *guarantee* that?" I asked him, cocking my head to one side. "Because I think I should tell you that I'm in it for the asparagus, and the fried chicken comes with potatoes. Not to mention the health benefits of the grill versus the slippery slope of God-only-knows what's in that frying oil."

He shook his head. "I'm just sayin' you look like you're not sure so I thought I'd help you out."

"Oh, I'm very sure," I said. "I. Like. Asparagus."

"Suit yourself," he said. "Don't say I didn't warn you."

I had to give him credit. It was the worst pickup line ever, and in addition, I looked like I did and he was still trying. If this was the lame adventure the Universe had in store for me, and he was single, I at least had to see it through. It can't be worse than Squirmy or Grumpy Perv.

I put my hand over his to make the connection complete.

"I take full responsibility and I appreciate your dedication to strangers' food choices. You don't see that much anymore," I said, as graciously as I could.

"Oh, but I have a vested interest," he said, matter-of-factly, perking back up. "I'm the poultry satisfaction manager of this restaurant. It's my job to connect people with the right chicken." I giggled, making his solidarity wink at the bartender ineffective at best.

The chicken came, lickety-split, and he got up to leave.

"Oh," I teased, "you're not even going to watch to see if I wretch? After all, you did *guarantee* it." I gave him a doe-eyed look, just to punctuate the invitation.

"Are you sure you want me to see that?" he asked, as he tossed a wave at his buddies and sat back down.

"I would appreciate it if you would give the asparagus a chance." I handed him a fork, and dared him to eat.

His friends interrupted a minute later.

"Hey, man, you ready? We gotta go." My nameless friend rose from his stool and looked at me apologetically.

"You're leaving me *now?* You come in here, with your fancy talk of chicken, share my meal and then you just *up and leave?* Are you kidding me?" I ranted as indignantly as I could. "Man, I can't believe you!" I shook my head at him dramatically and went back to my meal.

He smirked, and turned to the guys. "Can we meet up with you when she's finished eating?"

As I finished my dinner, my companion told me about his job as a high school basketball coach, and how he liked to be active in his community, but that he was considering moving on. "It's time for me to make some real money," he said finally.

"Why? Are you in debt? Because it sounds like you're very happy where you are. Most people don't find that kind of satisfaction from their work."

"Oh no, I'm quite comfortable. I have a house, a car, and the ability to contribute to causes that I believe in, you know, to make the world a better place. I have everything I need. I just feel like it's time to do something more, something different."

When the bill came, he stood up, and reached into his pocket. I noticed for the first time that he was tall. I mean, *very* tall. I was on the petite side, but I think I maybe came up to his belly button. I stopped him.

"I don't remember you asking me out, Paul Bunyan," I winked, and paid the check with a large bill I'd tucked in my pocket earlier in case of a far-away emergency.

"Oh, Miss Independently Wealthy," he snickered, and asked what I did that allowed me to toss big bills around like that.

"Whatever I want," I said, my new, perfect go-to answer, and lately what I needed to hear myself say.

"Well, that must be very nice," he replied, and invited me to join him and his friends at the bar where they were waiting for him.

Chapter 23

Paul Bunyan

The bar was loud, and his friends were getting loaded, but Paul Bunyan and I played skee ball and chatted all evening. I enjoyed listening to him as he told me about his family—brothers-and-sisters, thank God, not wife-and-kids—his job, aspirations, and how important he thought it was to be kind and generous, and pay back the community, which was probably bullshit, but reinforced my decision to call him Paul Bunyan. Finally, he noticed the conversation was one-sided.

"But you haven't told me much of anything about you. C'mon, Pretty Girl. What's your name? What do you really do?"

"I'm a writer," I said, matter-of-factly, ignoring the name question. *Well, I am*, I argued silently to myself. *I just don't collect a paycheck for it.*

This seemed to stop him in his tracks. "Really?" he asked incredulously, "What do you write?"

I considered the question for a minute before I replied, "All kinds of stuff. Articles, books, whatever needs to be written." I hadn't thought about my subject matter. All I knew was that I'd always wanted to be a writer, and now was my chance to get away with it.

"What kinds of books?"

I scrambled. "I'm working on a teen romance," I said, reasoning in my head that he wouldn't be interested enough to have any further questions. "Big market for that right now." As the words came out, I felt myself come alive. There was no turning back. *I am a writer.* My mind wandered off to a corner of my bedroom with a laptop and a stack of manuscripts I could see in my head.

"Have I heard of you?"

"I'm not on the best-seller list right now, if that's what you're asking." *See, I didn't lie,* I told myself, becoming even more confident in my new identity.

"That is so cool." Paul Bunyan suddenly had a new respect for me, and he looked a little deeper into my eyes. "They're gorgeous," he said, "you know that?"

"Thank you," was all I said. I do happen to know; it's my one good feature that people have commented on since I was a little girl. But I do love it when boys think they're the first to discover them, as if nobody ever looked at my face or heard of eyeballs before. And after last night with the Perv, I was beginning to wonder myself.

I asked him how long he was required to stay at the bar with his friends. It had been a long day of solitary pursuit, and I wanted to know if it was going to end in my favor. I actually really liked this guy.

"They're all staying at my place tonight. I drove."

My heart sank while I tried to shuffle up my game. "Oh, too bad," I said, expecting yet another miserable ending, but going down swinging anyway. "I was hoping you'd walk me back to my hotel room."

That got the ball rolling. It didn't take long for him to tie up the loose ends of giving up his keys and letting the guys know where he'd be. I kissed each of his friends goodbye and told them I hoped I didn't put a kink in their plans. Then, the tall, generous Minnesota folk hero and I were off.

We walked what seemed the long way back to the hotel, but maybe it was just the heat, combined with Paul Bunyan's exponentially longer strides than I could make in my now-worn flip-flops, which were clearly just for show. After a few blocks of yanking on his arm, he finally adjusted his gait. I thought he'd be used to that sort of thing by this point in his life, but apparently he wasn't much of a walker.

Along the way, we passed, for lack of a better term, a couple of street gangs that had collected on one corner or another; nothing menacing, and my new friend knew at least one kid in every group. He would explain that he'd met this kid at the Y summer program where he coached a pickup league or something, or how that kid got shot and he was helping him to catch up on his studies. This further cemented for me the mythically tall, do-gooder name of Paul Bunyan for my companion, and now it was time for a mythical adventure.

We finally arrived at Room 1801, my junior suite on the top floor of the hotel, and Paul Bunyan was clearly impressed. I could tell that he was wondering if I was J.K. Rowling or something. I pulled out the card key and slid it through the opening, but when the green light approved our entrance, he hesitated.

"Are you just going to stand there, or are you coming in?" I heard myself say with my newly-discovered voice of a come-hither vixen. *Writers are sexy!*

Paul Bunyan had to shake himself, but he recovered and, with wide eyes, followed me into the room.

I didn't know what I was going to do next, but I did know that this guy was not leaving without a story for his friends, nor was I. I was ready for anything, even if I had to recall my Lamaze breathing to do it.

I took him by the hand, kicked off my flip-flops and jumped on the bed, where, standing upright, I could now finally look him straight in his big, brown eyes. I pulled him close, and kissed him.

"You're really hot, you know that?" he panted.

"It's 100 degrees out," I purred.

"It feels so much hotter in here," he whispered, running his hands down my back.

"It's about to get hotter," I said, as I pulled away. I wanted to stay right there, but I needed something more. I fixed my eyes on him, and let the words tumble out, not knowing where they were headed. "How about we clean up before we get dirty?" I asked, and began shucking my sweat-drenched clothes in a sticky striptease. His eyes lit up like fireflies as I clarified, "I'm going to take a shower. Would you care to join me?"

Paul Bunyan wasted no time in getting rid of his jeans and Polo shirt. He scooped me up and spun me around, looking for the bathroom door. We slid across the marble floor and into the shower, and as we pressed against the cool tiles and adjusted the water colder and colder still, all I could think of was how much fun this was, steaming up the joint with body heat. And that I hadn't appreciated soap this much since Crayola made color bubble bath.

Eventually, Paul Bunyan turned off the water and wrapped me in a thick, plush hotel towel. He carried me to the bed, and unraveled the towel, brushing his face with it one last time before he tossed it on the floor and stood over me, hungry, considering his next move.

He lowered himself on top of me, and kissed me with everything he had. He was by turns intense and playful, and I wanted so much to be with him, but he had yet to make a move for his wallet. Finally, I had to ask him if he brought any protection with him.

The poor guy looked like a bus ran over his dog when he came up empty, but I shook my head in response. "There's a dress code to get in here," I said as I pushed him away in frustration. And then I began to laugh. "Are you telling me that you planned a night out at a club with the guys, and you don't have a condom in your wallet? That's Rule Number One, genius."

"But I drove," he protested, "I have stuff at home."

"At the frat house?" I had to make fun of him now; it was just too easy. I knew, when he began to laugh along with me, that I liked him for a reason, but it was getting late, and he began to creep into a spoon position for what he thought would be an overnight cuddle, which was Mistake Number Two. Who wants to wake up with a stranger? I had decided several months earlier that there would never be a sleepover, not only for the awkwardness of decidedly less-hot morning breath, but also because my state of mind was fragile, and by not allowing them, I would significantly reduce the chance of remorse the next day.

"Hey buddy," I had to shake him, "you gotta get dressed."

"Wha?" He was already half-asleep.

"No sleepovers. You gotta go home."

He blinked his eyes open. "Are you serious? You want me to leave?"

"No sleepovers. Sorry—policy. Get your clothes on."

"But I don't have my car. I gave it to the guys."

"That's why God made taxis. Get up."

Poor Paul Bunyan. No condoms, no sex, not even a cuddle, and now he was hopping on one foot, trying to get his leg in a pair of jeans that had turned inside-out in his earlier haste to remove them. I helped him straighten them out, and then I backed him out of the door.

"Send me a text and let me know you got home safely. It's late."

He looked at me first with venom, and then with a smirk that suggested he thought he was getting punk'd, but he did as he was told, and when the door closed, he knocked. I opened the door and his puppy dog eyes were so hopeful. I gave him a really nice, long kiss, taking his hand and dragging it along the curves of my body, and whispered, "Maybe next time you'll be more responsible. Goodnight." I closed the door, and that was the last I'd planned on seeing Paul Bunyan. I felt an enormous sense of power in the sexy woman I had just become; and that as much as I liked him, I wasn't afraid to stand my ground.

After I brushed my teeth and settled into bed, I texted him: Home yet?

He replied: Just pulled up. Goodnight.

The time was 4:13 a.m. I went right to sleep. I'd had my little adventure, a new text number, and a plane to catch in a few short hours.

Chapter 24

Boys of Summer

My stranger etiquette kicked in again during the transit ride to the airport, and I texted Paul Bunyan: I apologize for kicking you out. Nothing personal, just a policy I have.

He didn't respond for a day or two, or maybe even three, but around the fourth day back at the cottage with the kids, I looked at my texts and was surprised to find, buried among thirty picture texts from Squirmy chronicling his vacation to the Cayman Islands, and a few texts from the Perv about my ass, there was a text from Paul Bunyan that said simply: What's the policy?

It made me smile to see that he responded, but it wasn't exactly urgent, so I forgot about it and went back to preparing for a night of s'mores and catching fireflies, on one of those perfect summer evenings that get stuck in our core memories that I'd hoped the kids would look back on and believe that every summer night of their childhood was just like this one.

I had a renewed appreciation for my children and our time together. We had struggled through a couple of years of my apathy and detachment, but that summer was the one I had consciously claimed back for us. We were blessed with the tiny summer cottage that served our desire to be together in the safety of our "summer family," friends, and neighbors whom we never saw but for the slice of time we spent in the warm breezes, cool waters, and bright stars that set the scene for skinned knees, freckled noses, and toothless smiles. It was heaven, and although I no longer had a mate, I had all of that, and I wasn't lonely there.

Still, I loved the idea of testing my limits, meeting people, and finding adventures. I was energized by the ways I was connecting to people, especially men, on different levels, and I was experiencing a growth in my ideas about who I was, and who I was becoming. It could have been the romance of summer itself, but I felt better than I had in decades, and because I was so grateful to have a second chance at life, a new phase, my Saturn return or whatever else it was, I wasn't going to waste it.

Later that evening, after the kids went to bed, and I'd considered some witty answers, I decided short and to the point was the best response to Paul Bunyan: No sleepovers. Ever.

It took him another couple of days, and another couple dozen pictures of sea turtles and exotic birds from Squirmy, plus a night of Perv's sexting, to get his next message: What's the reason for this policy?

I had to take a few minutes to laugh at myself. It was the middle of the summer, I had been dumped by a jilted home-improvement salesman, which led to being stalked by a nature-loving photographer and sexted by a pervert—neither of whom I would ever see again—and I was excited to get a six-word text from an almost-one-night stand who was still using the high school handbook for boys who want to talk to girls. It was ridiculous.

I ignored his question and asked him instead: Is it still the rule that you have to wait at least two days to text a girl so she won't think you're too interested?

Before the end of the day, he had haha'd me and followed it with: Yes, I work in a high school, that's how we roll. Then he added: What's the reason for the policy?

I giggled in spite of myself.

I sleep better was all I replied.

Hungry for all the attention my ego could get, and assured of always getting a response, I continued texting Squirmy and the Perv. The photo-stalking Squirmy texted all day, from anywhere he was. He was really enjoying the attention of his mystery text gal, an obvious novelty for him. For my part, I responded to every photo with a *Wow! Cool!* or, *So Beautiful!* or something similar, so I wouldn't sound like I was on auto-answer, but with dozens of photos of wildlife, and no interesting commentary, it was a challenge.

Perv always texted me at night, obviously because he was a pervert who was probably hiding in the basement bathroom or something; and he always wanted to have a *Penthouse Forum* chat. I felt bad that he had to resort to texting a complete stranger just to get a little attention (hello, pot calling kettle!), so I tried to give him what I could just to boost his ego. I would respond to most of his texts with the welcome but generic *that's so hot* or *that feels good* or anything else that sounded like I was engaged in his fantasy, but mostly, it just seemed icky. I felt like a *Saturday Night Live* skit: a woman answering the sex lines while she's shooing kids and cooking burritos with her hair in curlers, but that's about what it amounted to, so whenever I caught myself rolling my eyes when he would tell me he was imagining me with fishnet stockings and fuck-me pumps, and wanting to rub oil all over me, I tried to tease him a little so at least one of us would feel better. It was painful to know that bored as I was, this was what this guy looked forward to, and if he needed me this badly, well, it was the least I could do for him. It wasn't the pervy part that bothered me; it was that he felt uncared-for. I felt this was my way of honoring what I'd told him in the beginning: *I don't hold it against you.* And I didn't. It was a way to let him know that he was loved, just as he was. Even if only by a curler-clad, burrito-making mama.

And so it went. Each night after I put the kids to bed and cleared the exotic birds from my data plan, I would wonder if I would hear from Paul Bunyan, only to get the Perv texting for an hour. And attention whore that I was, I'd let him drag me into another night describing my nurse's uniform or cheer-leading skirt, and sure enough, just when the Perv needed me to text my *oh, babys* most, Paul Bunyan would chime in, and I would turn my attention to him. I began to look at Perv as the gateway to Paul Bunyan, because it was so predictable.

Paul Bunyan, on the other hand, was witty and charming and, once I called him out on the every-other-day business, I began to hear from him most evenings after the warm up act from Perv. We texted small talk at first, but our banter was so easy that we quickly found ourselves right where we'd left off in Minneapolis. I decided that since he responded well to candid questions and because who knew if we'd ever see each other again, I had nothing to lose by being honest and shooting straight with him—except, of course, with any personal information. I found that it was so much easier to be honest with my feelings when I wasn't worried about someone Googling me and asking me questions about my old life—or X's, which was the life I'd dissolved into for so many years and from which I was trying to extricate myself. I was here, now:

new life, new adventures, new possibilities, new truths. Even if I was only making them up as I went along, they fit better than the old act I had been performing for so many years.

It didn't take very long before we concluded that we needed to see each other again. I knew I wanted to spend more time with Paul Bunyan. He was kind and playful, smart and lighthearted. I wanted to have a conversation with him longer than a few text bubbles at a time, which was unusual for me, because I generally saw more of people in the words I read off my little phone than most people could see over the course of an evening on a dinner date.

I knew he wanted to see me again, too. I mean, I couldn't discount the fact that he had left that night with an unfinished conquest. He needed to complete the job, tell his friends the end of the story, whatever. But I could tell there was a part of him that really just wanted to hang out with me, too. We texted a lot about sex; but just as often, he would begin an evening's conversation wanting to know why I chose the car I drove or my opinion on whether math skills were more important than language skills. He was interesting to me on so many levels, and I was still missing the mental stimulation I had so appreciated from 390, so in keeping with my honesty policy, I took a deep breath and suggested that it was his turn to visit me.

He had lots of excuses. This was the one thing I loved about all of my text boyfriends. They all thought everything was impossible until I'd point out how possibility worked. I was in the midst of discovering that when I would focus on Love, Adventure, and Possibility, the Universe brought me Opportunity, and I wasn't going to wait until conditions were right for him. I'd learned the hard way that, depending on your perspective, conditions are never right. Or always right. All my children were born in distress situations, and my entire life up until that point—certainly the last few years—had pretty much felt like a distress situation. My kids were incredible, my life was just getting interesting, and I'd decided that possibility was the only way of life for me now.

I'm solution driven, I told him, and asked him to choose a time for me to come back to Minneapolis.

Chapter 25

Airport Delay

t was the last weekend of the summer, the one before Labor Day, and X had the kids for the week. I packed up the summer cottage, headed to the mall for school supplies, ignoring the weather reports of a hurricane due that weekend, and went home to pack for Minneapolis.

The morning of the trip, Kali texted me. What are you going to wear?

I had nothing to lose on this trip. The guy had met me at my worst. Anything beats sweat-soaked jeans and a workout t-shirt, so I decided to go for it all at once and put on a long, white, flowing skirt; a tight, white t-shirt; and bright red, high-heeled Jimmy Choo sandals.

Goddess outfit. Kali approved, and I set off for the airport.

As I waited for my flight to board, a handsome man strode up to me and handed me his card.

"You're not by chance going to Kansas City, are you?" he asked nervously, and when I shook my head, he took a deep breath and said. "My flight's leaving in a few minutes, but I can't get on the plane without telling you how stunning you are."

Stunning. The word was enough to make me blush, yet it empowered me with more confidence than I'd ever felt. Only six months before, I'd been thirty-five pounds heavier and on antidepressants. Now a complete stranger felt the need to tell me I was stunning. And I felt it. I smiled at him, and looked at his card. Special Agent. *Hmm,* I thought, *a superhero.*

"Is this your cell number?" I asked with a devilish grin, and stored it in my contacts for future reference.

"Call me anytime," he winked, and he turned toward his gate and headed down the jetway.

I took out my phone as the door closed behind him, and texted him a smiley face. Very nice to meet you and continued on to my flight.

The Minneapolis airport was bigger than I'd remembered, and I spent a good deal of time trying to figure out exactly where I would exit for the big rendezvous with Paul Bunyan, when my cellphone buzzed.

Just landed and can't stop thinking of you. Who are you? It was a text from the Special Agent.

I giggled to myself and smiley-faced him. Then I turned my attention to the matter at hand.

The phone rang, which startled me. I looked at it, hoping it wasn't X with some emergency, since he had no idea where I was for the weekend. It wasn't. It was Paul Bunyan.

"Helloooo?" I answered in the most lyrical voice I could muster, only slightly freaked out that this was the first time he'd ever voice-dialed me. It may seem odd to some, but for me it was perfectly natural that all my relationships lately were text-based.

"I'm so sorry. So sorry," he said, and my heart dropped. Before I could digest the words that meant he was cancelling on me, he continued, "I wanted to be there when you came out. I wanted to hold up a sign to welcome you. I wanted to see you right when you arrived."

I didn't say anything because I was a goddess today, a *stunning* goddess, and I didn't want to be angry, so I waited for the excuse. I could book a flight to Kansas City and spend the weekend with a superhero if necessary, but I would not allow the weekend to be ruined.

"I'm five minutes away, but there is construction, and it might take me more like fifteen minutes. Do you mind waiting?"

I scrunched up my face, at the same time relieved he was still coming, and annoyed that he would initiate a panic that gave me flashbacks of the Wisconsin Weasel from my last trip.

"I'm not even sure where I should meet you," I recovered, "there are so many places to exit."

"I'll let you know when I'm close to the airline door," he said, and we both hung up.

You can slap me if you want. Sorry, 5 minutes came the text a minute later.

I will reserve the option, thank you. I pecked back.

Can't wait to see you. 2 minutes. He was already flustered.

It had been over a month since I saw him, and while all my text boyfriends felt the need to send me text photos of themselves and parts of themselves, Paul Bunyan was the exception. I liked him for the way he made me feel, so it never occurred to me to classify him in physical terms. He was dark, handsome, and very tall, I certainly knew that, but would I remember him from inside the car as he drove up? I decided not to take the chance.

What kind of car are you driving? I texted.

White Lexus he replied instantly, as if he knew what I was thinking. Then, What are you wearing?

I had to laugh at that one, because whenever we had a

heated text exchange about anything, he would just redirect with that golden nugget, and we would change the subject back to sex. Excellent ploy, proven results.

Red shoes was all I gave him.

Chapter 26

Romance in the Air

The white Lexus was still rolling to a stop as the driver side door opened, and I could see Paul Bunyan's arm curl up on top of the roof to help support him as he lifted his extra-tall body out of the car in his haste to greet me. He was more handsome than I remembered, and I was relieved that my heatstroke on the night of our initial meeting hadn't affected my visual faculties. I waited patiently as he made his way around the car, muttering apologies for his tardiness, opened the back door, took my bag and set it neatly on the backseat, and turned his attention to me.

"Finally," he said, as he scooped me into his arms, his nervousness and mine dissolving at once. He kissed me sweetly on the cheek, then smiled mischievously and said, "I love your shoes."

We settled into the car, and I tried to be quiet while he negotiated his way through the airport construction. When he was confidently back on familiar roads, he asked casually, "Where would you like to go first?"

I giggled at him, because he knew darned well where I wanted to go, and I was only visiting for 24 hours. Instead, I said, "What have you got planned?" Then, after a pause, added, "I'm thinking the pharmacy might be a good bet," breaking the ice and teasing him about his lack of preparation the last time we were together.

"I would very much like to check you into the hotel right now," he said, reaching over the console and taking my hand and weaving his fingers through mine, "but it occurred to me that if we go there first, we probably won't leave until check-out time tomorrow."

"And you would rather introduce me to your mother?" I asked sarcastically.

"You look very pretty," he said seriously. "Even more than I remembered." Then he returned to his thoughts and continued, "I'd like for you to see a little bit of my city. Is there anything in particular you'd like to see?"

"As long as I get to see my tour guide naked before my next flight, I'm open to seeing the sights. How many of the nine thousand, nine hundred ninety-nine lakes that I haven't seen can we take in before then?"

He laughed. "Oh, I will definitely show you a lake or two. But first, there is something I would like you to see." He pulled into a vacant lot so riddled with potholes that I was afraid he was going to get a concussion from his head hitting the roof of the car, so I asked him where the nearest hospital was, just in case I had to take over. He pulled the car to a stop somewhere in the middle of the lot, as if he could see invisible markings on the pavement showing him where to park, and looked at me with a big smile.

"It's fantastic!" I squealed, fully aware that my sense of adventure really fucked me up sometimes, and yet I was always willing to go with it. "How'd you discover this place?"

He laughed at me, and came around to help me out of my side of the car. It wasn't easy to steady myself on uneven asphalt in five-inch heels, so I did my best to pretend I really wanted to walk closely with him, and not just use his arm for balance.

"Alright, now, just give me a chance," he said, with an exasperated look that was a million times more adorable than the *now-we're-too-far-away-for-anyone-to-hear-you-scream* look which I was fully expecting, since I could see no other reason why we would be in this desolate location.

We walked to the edge of the lot, where Paul Bunyan guided me to a tiny path between two cypress trees. As if by magic, there emerged on the other side a beautiful lush of greenery, the backdrop to an unexpected sculpture garden. It was wide open, with manicured lawns and gravel, stone, and brick pathways that led to the various installations. Right in the middle of the lawn, on its own little island surrounded by tall, wavy grasses, with the Minneapolis skyline in the background, stood the unofficial symbol of the city. I remembered it right away from the book in my hotel room the last time I'd been there: a giant spoon with a cherry balancing on top. It was beautiful and whimsical, and I immediately appreciated Paul Bunyan's thoughtful effort to bring me there, to set the tone for a no-pressure night of fun.

He flagged down some Asian tourists and handed them his cellphone, gesturing toward me.

"It's our wedding day," he said loudly to them, "that's my bride, all in white. Will you photograph us for our future children to see?"

The Asians obliged, and the photo was taken from so far away as to get everything in it, that even after he forwarded it to me, I still wouldn't know what Paul Bunyan looked like except by memory.

After a stroll through the garden, we returned through the looking glass and back into the Lexus.

"Now," he asked, "how about a lake?"

Paul Bunyan and I chatted easily while he drove through the familiar neighborhood where I was sure I'd nearly died on a bicycle the month before, just hours before I met him. I thought of how comfortable I was here, as a glamorous, confident woman with only a first name and not a care in the world, taking in the sights of a strange city with a handsome lover. It was a feeling I'd only read about in novels, and never knew existed in real life, certainly not back at home. I liked this woman. She was free and easy, beautiful and real. Why couldn't I be her all the time? I made a mental note to be her at least more often.

Instead of stopping at Lake Calhoun, Paul Bunyan took a few more turns and wound his way through an affluent neighborhood with dramatic floral landscaping against enormous, regal homes. He slowed the car in front of some of his favorites, and as voyeurs, we spied through the picture windows to admire the artwork and furnishings of the occupants.

Eventually, he parked the car and turned his attention across the street. There, right in the middle of the neighborhood, was a tiny, bona fide lake, complete with stone pedestrian bridges and platform docks. It was so picturesque, I had to take a few moments to soak it all in. Everywhere we looked, silent but active kayakers, cyclists, swimmers, and joggers seemed to flow through the scenery like ribbons flowing through the wind.

He took my arm and we walked around the path that hugged the Lake of the Isles. It was a warm night, with a light breeze that blew kisses of cool air at us, and we arrived at the platform dock just in time to sit on a bench and watch the sun set, in colors I would remember long after the spoon and cherry picture was erased from my iPhone.

It was so romantic, sitting across his lap, my head resting on his shoulder, my long skirt trailing over the bench, talking easily and then instinctively hushed as the bright orange ball got bigger and lower in the sky until it finally disappeared behind the trees and, as the last ray of light disappeared over the horizon, Paul Bunyan lifted my head and kissed me so tenderly, so passionately, it took my breath away.

It would have been so easy to stay there on that bench and make out until the warm night turned chilly, but my folk hero had class. When the moment had passed, he didn't try to prolong it; he simply stood up, wrapped his arms around me and said, "There isn't anyplace I'd rather be right now, than here with you. Thank you for being here, again."

As we walked back to the car, holding hands, all I could think was: *I want to be naked with this man very soon.*

Of course, Paul Bunyan had other plans.

"You must be starving. I haven't had a chance to feed you," he said.

"We could order room service," I replied, maybe a little impatiently.

"I've got one idea; if it falls through, we'll order in our bathrobes."

He took me to a French restaurant, and from the moment we stepped out of the car and onto the sidewalk, the air was filled with culinary aromas so enticing, I was willing to wait for a table. I guess I hadn't realized how hungry I really was, and I was glad he had allowed for it, because I would have hated to fall asleep from lack of nourishment without any action from this man.

We decided to sit at the wide, rounded bar, rather than wait for a table. We ordered a bottle of wine and shared a dish of risotto while sparring about the virtues of unrequited love. I can't remember if we concluded that one can or cannot make someone love another, but I do remember vividly how much I enjoyed that most romantic evening in such a very long time. Paul Bunyan was smart, funny, interesting and fun; not just in text, but a living, breathing, vibrant expression of love and life.

I couldn't figure out what was wrong with him.

To keep our one-name anonymity level agreement intact, something we immensely enjoyed—the idea that we could be anyone we wanted, and therefore our true selves, with no identifying information, only that which came directly from how we honestly felt in a given moment—I suggested that once we arrived at the hotel, he would park the car while I checked in. A few minutes later, I met him, red-faced at the elevator and he sheepishly told me that one of the valets had asked for the name of the hotel guest in order to store the car and receive a parking discount. When his face drew a blank, the two valets burst into laughter and gave him a high-five and each other a knowing look.

"Well, they're having a good laugh on us, anyway," I laughed, fully aware that in any other facet of respectable Real Life, it would have been humiliating. I kissed him lightly and reminded him that tonight, we could be anyone we wanted to be.

He sighed and finally let out a howl of laughter and agreed that when he retrieved the car, he would be the one smiling, and then he looked in my eyes and lovingly said, "And I'm unconcerned about the parking discount."

We entered the room, this one smaller and nothing like the one across the hall that we'd enjoyed on my last visit, and looked around to get our bearings. I put my bag down on a chair and went to wash my hands and apply some lip gloss.

When I returned, Paul Bunyan pointed to the window, and with a confused expression, said, "Check that out. The curtains are torn."

I followed his gesture, and saw that the window dressing had, indeed, been not just torn, but shredded as if a Bengal tiger had just checked out after room service had thrown a steak atop the curtain rod.

"I think you'd better call down and tell them we didn't do it," he said with a wink, "because we may not get to plead innocent tomorrow."

"Yeah, wait'll the valets hear about that one," I teased.

I called the front desk, cleared my throat and turned away from Paul Bunyan so he wouldn't hear my name through the phone, and awkwardly began, " Hi, I just checked in…"

The clerk on the other end of the line was appalled at my report, and asked if I'd like to be shown another room.

Just then, I felt him behind me. Silently, and without warning, Paul Bunyan was standing closer than a shadow, pressed against me. He reached his arms around me, and swept them up the front of my body with an urgency I could feel in his breath as he kissed my neck. He was everywhere, touching me, kissing me. A fire ignited inside me and I needed oxygen.

"Nevermind…" I whispered, as I dropped the receiver with a thud, and Paul Bunyan spun me around and lifted me to his lips, full of desire and unexpected force. My sandals dropped from my feet at that elevation, and we fell together on the fluffy, white cloud of a bed, the afternoon of romance turning swiftly and purposefully into a night of passion.

Paul Bunyan and I made every moment of our time together count. Every ounce of heat that had been bottled up for the last month had erupted in a thousand acts of physical affection, and it was only in the wee hours of the morning, as the sun streaked through the shredded shears, that he whispered, "Are you going to kick me out now?"

Chapter 27

Hurricane Season Begins

As Paul Bunyan and I waited for our brunch at the outdoor café the next morning, Kali sent a text: Are you alive?

I replied: Very much so, with a happy face.

Immediately, she texted back: Have you checked your flight? They're closing the airport. Hurricane coming.

I almost spit up my mimosa. There we were, sitting on an outdoor terrace, under an impossibly-blue sky, sun shining brightly, not a care in the world, and...*what?*

I checked the flight. It wasn't posted. I called the airline. There was a busy signal. A busy signal? My stomach knotted up. It had to be bad if I couldn't even get the automation. I called the hotel to see if I could extend my stay. They were booked solid with a convention, beginning today.

I looked nervously at Paul Bunyan. "What's up?" he asked.

"Nothing, it's just that I might have an issue with my flight. We should probably leave soon so I can get to the airport and straighten it out."

"That's perfect," he said, "as much as I hate to see you go, I have to get to work and set up my office. School starts next week and I have a ton of stuff I've been putting off. But I'm glad I did this time," he grinned at me.

I watched with a smile as Paul Bunyan retrieved his car from the parking valet at the hotel, and after he opened my door for me, he walked back to his side, where the valet waited by the door for a tip, then pressed his hand into Paul Bunyan's with a barely audible, "yeah, man," and pulled it back for a low-five. I waved to the valet, and he said, "I'll remember you when you come back."

We arrived at the airport, and after he gathered my bag from the backseat, Paul Bunyan took my hands in his, and looked into my eyes with a gentle admonishment to call him if I had any trouble with my flight.

"Twenty-four hours, that was our deal," I said. "I'll see you next time, whenever that will be." I kissed him, and he swept me up in a hug, and I felt so warm and tingly, and yet again, so empowered by not confusing a light, romantic whirlwind with a heavy, new boyfriend.

I didn't need to watch him go; I had to figure out how I was going to get home, because X was going to be dropping the kids off the next day. I took my place in the long line of weary travelers, and tossed around contingency plans in my head.

When it was my turn, I smiled as warmly as I could, given the panic that had been building as I waited, and said to the customer service representative, "Hi, I know that the weather isn't your fault, and I know that everyone has to be somewhere…"

She held up her hand as she looked at my boarding pass. "Stop," she said. "Every airport within 100 miles of your destination will be closed over the next hour. Air traffic is landing everyone currently in the air, and then that's it until the hurricane passes, hopefully in the next 24 to 48 hours. But I wouldn't count on getting out even then; all the flights have to be made up, and we're trying our best to squeeze people onto already-full flights. Best to wait until the day after tomorrow to let it all get sorted out, so you won't be cancelled or delayed again if the weather lingers."

I was dumbfounded. I didn't even know what to ask next. I stared at her, my mouth open, my eyes wide with oncoming tears, panic setting in wondering what I would tell X.

The woman continued, more gently this time, "Ma'am, I suggest you go back to wherever you're staying, and wait it out. It's beautiful here; take a walk in the park. But don't come back until you call us and get a confirmed flight so you don't have to sit around here, getting cranky." With that, she motioned me to step aside, and called for the next passenger in line.

Dazed, I left the line, and like a cartoon, I turned back once, twice, as if I had just remembered a question, but then trudged on, knowing what the answer would be. I texted Kali: Some adventure!

She texted back: What are you going to do now?

I had no idea.

Grudgingly, I texted Paul Bunyan. I hated to do it, because our time together was so perfect, you couldn't have orchestrated that kind of chemistry if a blockbuster movie depended on it; but it was only meant to be for a day, and I liked to make my exit before I overstayed my welcome.

Hang tight, he texted back, I'll come get you.

He arrived less than a half-hour later, and I explained the situation to him, leaving out the day-after-tomorrow timetable. I was still holding out hope that I'd be on a plane and back home before bedtime the next night.

"Great," he said. "I'd love for you to see my house. I'll have to let my roommate know that you're coming, but you're more than welcome and I'm happy to have you, and I'll get you back to the airport first thing in the morning."

Oh, right. The frat house. I'd forgotten that he had a roommate and I'd just remembered that I didn't have any other clothes with me; the idea was to electrify and exit like the sophisticated woman I had become; not hang around in a borrowed t-shirt like a sorority girl after pledge week.

"I've still got a whole day's worth of work to do, and I can't take you to my office, because it's security-monitored. But there's a nice park around the corner, and you can enjoy the day, and hang out at the café across the street if you're hungry. They have wi-fi so you can check the flights." With that, he was off, with my overnight bag in the backseat, and I was left with my cellphone and little else.

It was useless to call the airline; their phone lines and website were frozen from overuse, so I texted Kali the details of our evening, and then my cellphone gave me the low-battery warning, so I texted Paul Bunyan to let him know that I didn't have a charger with me. He gave me a landmark and an estimated time to meet him, and I signed off and went for a walk around one of the loveliest parks near the river, and tried my best to enjoy the day.

He was as gracious as ever when he returned to collect me, and we grabbed a table nearby and had a bite before we took another walk along the river. He looked uneasy.

"Listen," I said. "I know this is completely unexpected, and I do not expect to hold you to your offer. You can take me back to the airport if you want, no hard feelings."

"It's not that. I told you I'd love to have you over to my place, and I really mean it. Besides, I'm not going to let you wait out a hurricane in the airport."

"Then what is it? Something is bothering you."

"Well," he stammered, "I don't know how…"

"Just spit it out, Bunyan. No judgment."

He let out a high-pitched laugh like it was contained in a hot-air balloon, and cleared his throat. "It's just that I have a date tomorrow night, and I've been trying to get together with this girl for a month, and it's my only shot. If your flight doesn't leave until…"

I joined him, and let out a howl of my own. "Double booked? You're kidding!"

"Well, who would have thought your flight would get cancelled for weather in the middle of the best summer we've ever had here? Besides, this is a fantasy; it's not like I expect you to come back every weekend, and I'd like to find a nice girl who lives in the same time zone."

We laughed together for a few minutes at our predicament, and then he cleared his throat and said seriously, "I'm sorry. That's really ungentlemanly of me."

I took his hand and weaved my fingers through his, as he'd done when he picked me up at the airport. "You know what I like best about you? Your honesty. I think it's awesome that you and I understand and trust each other enough to talk about this."

He gave me a bear hug, which felt comfortable and familiar by now, and then he took me to his house, where we made homemade scones and played Scrabble until bedtime. We had another incredible night together, but this time, in place of the previous night's passion, there was genuine, loving trust in our kinship. We fell asleep together, wrapped securely in each other's arms, with no hint of the irony of our circumstance.

The storm blew through the East Coast, and the airport opened later the next day. Paul Bunyan dropped me at the departure door one final time with another heartfelt hug and the sweetness of a kiss I'd never forget, along with the leftover scones we'd made the night before.

I was able to get on the last flight out, but since I wouldn't be home at the agreed-to time, I called X, ready to confess that I'd been away on a date. It turned out that he had taken the kids on a road trip to visit his relatives and had gotten caught in the weather restrictions as well. He wouldn't be back with the kids until well after I returned. I didn't even have to mention my fiasco!

I asked myself why I cared what X thought about my trip, and besides the obvious objection he would have to my adventure at his financial expense, the answer was that X was still in a fragile state, discussions of dividing assets were still hanging in the air, and I thought it unwise to open a hurtful can of worms while I was still trying to discover the answers as to why I needed to go away. Paul Bunyan was a fling, but X was still and always my partner, as the father of my children. I didn't want to lie, but I didn't want to confess to an affair that was already over, either. To do so would have been cruel. At least that's what I told myself.

What I refused to acknowledge was the greater fear of insecurity and inferiority that naturally surfaced around X. He had always called the shots; I had always let him, and because his name was on the paychecks, I always felt that he was entitled to do it. I was "just the mom," after all, and had no claim to "his" money for my own discretion. It seemed ridiculous to think of it that way, but my role had been clearly defined through the years. I wasn't sure I had rights outside of shepherding the children. But this venture I was on was more than just an ego trip. It was almost a primal need to go and discover who I was, outside of my role as a mother. Some people go on safaris or retreats; I was exploring myself through other peoples' eyes. I didn't know if I could have explained all that.

I wondered how things might have turned out had I told him about all of this from the start. Would it have laid the groundwork for a messy divorce, or would the high road of integrity have prevailed? Was there such a thing as a protective lie? How big would a half-truth need to be before it stopped masquerading as a little white lie? For reasons beyond my self-preservation and my ego, I would never know.

Chapter 28

Back to School

Back at home, things began to settle down. The kids were back in school, and I was on Mom Duty, 24/7. X was back to meetings and travel, messing up weekend schedules, and I was reduced to text-only, limited adventure in my days.

Perv was still texting, and as the school year got underway, it seemed he, too, had relaxed his all-out fantasy texts into a more disciplined routine. No longer texting late at night, he began texting before he headed into the office, and again in the afternoons. He began telling me stories about his children and asked about mine.

One day, he sent me a text that said, simply, Thank you.

For what? I replied.

For taking the time to respond to every text I send. I feel like you are the only one who listens to me, and that means a lot. You've become a true friend to me.

Whoa.

I had no idea that my new hobby could affect someone in any way other than as frivolous folly, and I felt suddenly awful for all the times I had demeaned him.

As if he were reading my thoughts, he added, I know I can be an ass, and I know that you don't care about my fantasies, but you still let me have them. That's why I think you're beautiful, even though I was drunk as hell when we met and don't really remember.

You're a good man, Perv, I replied, and then added, I'm happy that you trust me.

I really do, he texted back. Thank you.

After that, our text relationship shifted to more mundane issues: how much he hated his job, how much he loved his sons, and how much he wished he had more time to spend in his hot tub, with only the occasional naughty late-night text when he was feeling really lonely.

What is it you'd rather do? I asked him one day after he complained about his job again.

Not this, he replied.

Then stop doing it.

It pays the bills.

Then stop complaining about it.

He didn't respond for a couple of days, maybe even a week, and then I received this text: I used to be an artist. I always wanted to be an artist.

Then go paint.

I knew you'd say that.

An hour later sent me a picture of a pencil sketch, with the caption, I used to sell my charcoal prints before I got married.

It was lovely, and I told him, I think you could do it again.

I knew you'd say that, too, so I took my art supplies out of the garage.

Before I could respond, he followed up: Thank you.

Chapter 29

Marine Boy

thena has been my friend longer than anyone else in the world. We'd met at the age of three as our mothers passed on the street, and although our lives were, and had always been, drastically different, we managed to pick up where we'd left off each time we caught up. This was a friendship that was not based on anything in common—no DNA, no sorority, no shared interests—just fascination and admiration for how we each got through life. It was the purest relationship I'd ever had, the one that *just is.*

She called me as the school year was settling in, to tell me that she and her husband of one million years, and their teenage son, were picking up and moving to the Florida coast. No special reason, they just always had it in the plans and they finally decided there was no time like the present, and how soon could I come visit the guest room named in my honor?

I booked a flight for the next weekend I didn't have the kids, and I set off for the Sunshine State, knowing that somewhere in the next 24 hours, there would be some kind of an adventure. It so happened that the weekend I chose was also a big military weekend, with airshows over the ocean and Naval ships docked for tours. And weekend passes for enlisted men.

Athena and I left her men at home and went for a drink down by the water somewhere. It was early in the evening, the sun had just set, and we found an outside terrace almost completely empty, while everyone inside watched Florida college football games at the bar.

Across the deck sat two young, buzz-cut, sweatshirt-clad men, smoking cigarettes and drinking beers. They got up and gave us the once-over as they got refills, and I reminded the tall one, who had to be at least 6'2," that smoking would stunt his growth if he continued with the nasty habit. He smiled, and they slowly made their way back to their table, where he stubbed out his cigarette and they continued to watch us behind every sip of their red plastic cups.

On their next trip to the bar, they tried to be casual, but they were pacing too slowly for my taste, so when they leaned against the bar to place their order, I leaned into the tall one and asked, "Were you planning on just staring from all the way over there, or are you going to say something soon?"

He laughed and said sheepishly in a cute Southern drawl, "Aw, y'all caught us. We've got friends inside, but we were just trying to figure a way to talk to ya."

"It's not rocket science," I said. "Where are your friends?"

We followed them into a section of the bar where the group of six marines had a table and were ordering food. Athena and I joined them, and quickly divided them into the four who, like her, were either married or spoken for; and the two single lads for me to size up. Athena could talk to anyone and quickly had her four puppies shouting jokes and singing songs at the top of their lungs and playing drinking games without a hint of anyone getting into trouble. She took photos of each of them for security purposes, and tested all of their cellphone numbers so that should I disappear later, she would be able to track the culprit.

I already knew which of the two remaining gentlemen would be getting into trouble with me, so I patiently chatted with them about their rank in the Marines, and why they were on a ship but not in the Navy. Soon, it was quite clear to everyone that the tall one and I would be having an adventure. It was now just a matter of logistics.

Eventually the music began, and if there was one thing Athena enjoyed more than singing, it was dancing. She had the whole table on their feet in no time, except for the tall one, who looked at me and shook his head.

"I don't dance," he said.

"Me either," I said. "Let's go find something else to do."

He took my hand, satisfied that his commanding officer was at the bar and too preoccupied to notice, and we weaved our way around the dancing crowd and out into the parking lot.

Like a couple of patsies in a spy thriller trying to make a getaway, he asked urgently, "Do you have the keys to your friend's car?"

I laughed. "I am not making out with you in the backseat of a Prius."

"Shit," he deadpanned. "I can't even squeeze into the backseat of a Prius."

He scooped me up and kissed me hard, right in the middle of the parking lot, his face pressed fully and neatly on top of mine. He was hot and smoky and normally I might have wretched at the barroom odor, but combined with his musky scent and the warm salty breeze, not to mention the deadline we were on, I was perfectly willing to accept him, as is.

He spotted an unlocked, gated area beside the bar, an outside employee lounge, as it were, and carried me toward it.

His strides were getting longer, more decisive as he headed toward the employee break table leaning up against the brick wall of the bar. With great force, he pinned me up against the wall, where my shoulder hit a plastic box affixed to the bricks, and kissed me again, harder. Briefly, the lights on the patio dimmed, and when the force of his body against mine eased up, so did the lights. I had no idea how exciting it was to be manhandled like this! It was, quite literally, electrifying. For a moment, he pulled away, unsure of whether his advances were welcome. When he saw my big, wide smile, he pulled at me with more urgency, and pushed himself up against me, both of us against the wall, one hand protecting my head from certain destruction, the other—everywhere else.

He was all over me, rough, messy, wild. Rougher, messier, wilder. Insane.

By the time we had freed ourselves of the restraints of our clothing, two employees had come out for their break, staring open-mouthed at us. Undeterred, he threw me over his shoulder, and we disappeared toward the water, into the darkness of a wedge of unclaimed property behind the air-conditioning unit, to finish our mission. I had no idea that his kind of mayhem could be so enjoyable. It was at once frightening and exhilarating. I instinctively knew that he wouldn't harm me; yet Marine Boy had absolutely no control over his brute-force nature, and I was thrilled to be his target, careless or constructive, depending on one's viewpoint.

For a brief moment, I thought of how the adrenaline-fueled thrashing about might go terribly awry; but once detonated, Marine Boy became completely benign, and after a bit, helped me to my feet, and we got dressed. He walked me back into the bar, gently holding my hand, both of us brightly smiling. He presented me to Athena, and noticing the concern on her face, asked politely if we needed an escort to the car at this late hour. Athena declined but thanked him, threw a kiss to her minions, and we headed out the door, getting halfway home before I realized that my ID was missing. Athena was in a panic over the thought of an identity breach, but I was calm as we re-entered the parking lot. I knew I'd find it lying right where we shed our clothes an hour ago, next to the air-conditioner unit. I smiled at the thought, another adventure under my belt; careless, crazy, fun, and completely unexpected.

We'd only been out there for an hour together, but it had been plenty. We hadn't bothered to introduce ourselves. We both understood we weren't starting a relationship. I had a plane to catch; he had a ship's curfew before an open-sea mission. Thanks to Athena's security measures, I was able to send him a text before he lost his signal in the Atlantic to thank him for a great night. He responded with a hope that we would meet again, and somewhere in his words, I saw that he was too young and angry to have all this *love-em-and-leave-em* in every port stuff down yet.

Although I do not recommend running off with men just met in a bar to anyone, and Athena had been understandably protective of me, she made a point to tell me she was proud of me.

"I've never seen you that far out of your mind," she laughed. "You've always played by the rules and I was always the one who found the trouble. Glad it finally rubbed off," she mused, as she simultaneously fist-bumped me and pointed the car toward the airport the next day.

"Like our own version of *Freaky Friday*," I agreed. I had to admit that it was a significant evening in that I had been open to an experience that was so far out of my comfort zone, and willing, just for the purpose of the experiment, to have enjoyed it fully.

The angry, rough sex I shared with Marine Boy that night was neither; it was quite a pleasant surprise to find that desire and energy were ignited within me in ways I never would have allowed before. I had been free to express myself openly, with a stranger for whom no judgment, nor consequence, would be registered. And that unlocked the chains of the ordinary, which allowed a new, more courageous me to emerge.

Chapter 30

Philadelphia Freakdom

The autumn leaves were falling, and I had my focus on the kids. X and I diligently worked on holiday arrangements, although we had still not hammered out anything resembling a divorce decree. It wasn't for any particular reason. We had been to a mediator, which did not work out the way we'd hoped, so we decided that the best thing we could do was to continue to operate as we were.

The thought of arguing over custody or money never really appealed to either of us; and because we focused all of our energy on the kids anyway, it was really as if nothing had happened, other than X moving out. Everything looked the same from the outside. We both showed up to school recitals and sports events, so what was the big deal? I knew I was in an experimental stage in terms of new relationships, so until he met the proverbial gold-digging girlfriend, I didn't really care about a divorce. I was looking for the love in all of it because it made me feel so much better, and I wanted to be at peace with the whole situation, which was becoming an open-marriage joke among my friends. I had been advised to think carefully about that irresponsible position. A new little hussy could cause him to leave me and the kids with nothing and that wouldn't be very peaceful, would it? I never really believed that, although these advisors sure scared the hell out of me on a regular basis.

It wasn't all roses for the kids, either. They had run their course with the therapist, and our summer had been so carefree and fun that I thought we were over the hump. But as it does, trouble began growing in school; discipline had become increasingly difficult; and general comprehension skills seemed to evade those ever-changing, always-evolving children of ours.

I found myself, after months of training myself to be "better" without antidepressants, and now completely off the pills and working diligently to wean myself off my own therapist, getting angry on a regular basis. It was something I had placed as a priority not to do, but which nevertheless had to be given its own space in creating our happy new home.

Perv was still texting, now about his kids and the art he had always wished to pursue. Paul Bunyan was keeping me informed on a new job he had taken in Chicago, the girl that hadn't worked out, and new prospects in romance. I had become his wingman, and we bantered about, with what would become decreasing regularity.

One chilly afternoon, I received a text from Squirmy, or *mdakfjarth,* the Harley-riding, wildlife-loving guy from the plane, saying he had business in Philadelphia, and would I like to meet him for dinner at a pub near the airport? I had forgotten that I had told him I lived in the area, but I was more than happy to spend a couple of hours in the car alone, certain that meeting him off my regularly beaten path would put me onto my next adventure—because what other purpose did he serve in my life? So I drove to Philadelphia and in my gross overestimation of travel time, I stopped to get a salad at one of those coffee and salad shops that were popping up all over, while I waited for our rendezvous hour.

The place was a little light on opportunities in the form of attractive people; however, one guy caught my attention simply by all his pacing. It was an odd sort of behavior in a public place, and he didn't seem to have any purpose for being there, so as my salad came over the counter, I looked for a spot as far away from the guy as possible, having that weird feeling that he was watching me out of the corner of his eye.

Somehow he was there in front of me, having some kind of psychotic conversation with himself that made him start and stop a number of times, so I looked directly at him and said simply, "Hello." Why I did that was beyond my understanding of the urges I got to do some of the things I did.

He stood in front of my table and opened his mouth to say something, but eventually closed back up. It was then that I noticed the earmuffs.

He was wearing wraparound earmuffs with a Philadelphia Flyers logo, bright orange and frayed, and looking completely ridiculous on the head of a grown man with a ponytail, for myriad reasons, not the least of which was, well, Philadelphia Flyers.

Hockey was beginning to haunt me. Turnpike Steve had been a hockey fan; Big Bald Billy had repeatedly mentioned his work with a hockey legend; and out of the blue, my kids decided to take up hockey, having no family history or prior understanding of the sport. This was the sign that I wasn't necessarily looking for, but there it was, and I didn't want to acknowledge it.

"If you're a Flyers fan, just keep walking," I said, as I speared my fork through a huge green leaf of lettuce and shook my head at the Universe.

"Oh, come on," he said, as he took the opportunity to grab a chair from the next table and positioned it across from me. "Don't be hating on Philly," he said. "Obviously, you're not from around here."

"Good guess, Detective," I said. "If you plan on sitting down, you'd better plan on removing the muffs."

"Oh, really? Why, who am I up against? The Penguins?"

"Not your concern; just take off the muffs or move down a seat."

To my surprise, he moved down a seat. "What, Rangers? Bruins? Caps?" He tried again from the next table.

"Okay, let's have it," I said, putting my fork down. "What do you want?"

"Huh? Me? What do I *want?*" He asked with a flair, as he spread his palm and all of his fingers open across his chest.

"Oh, great, a drama queen," I said, rolling my eyes. "What's your story, princess?"

Philly Muff took a minute to switch gears. Finally, after drawing his thumb and forefinger to his chin a few times, and opening and closing his mouth like a singing bass, he said, "I just got some really good news, and I'm kinda trying to process it."

"Oh, good for you!" I squealed, as I lifted my fork and all the greenery on it in his direction.

"Don't you want to know what I'm celebrating?"

"Not particularly. If it makes you happy, then I'm happy," I said, and I toasted him with my cup of hot tea.

He looked at me with a cocked head and said, "Well, maybe I don't wanna tell you."

"All the better," I said, "but clearly you do, so spill it. Make it fast, Muff Daddy."

"I just got good news is all," he tried to sound coy. "It's about my health."

"Your health is everything, so congratulations," I said, much less enthusiastically, and probably with spinach in my teeth.

"Well, no it's not," he countered, "but in this case…" he trailed off. Eventually he returned his attention to the conversation and said, "It's just good news I wasn't expecting."

"Well, I certainly wasn't expecting it either, but here you are so enough already. Either tell me your good news story, or move along with your bad news earmuffs." I was getting bored with his attempts to create a buzz around himself, and I was annoyed with myself for my lack of patience in waiting out a better prospect and getting stuck with this one. But as I'd learned by now, I loved me some unexpected acquaintances, and all it took was a little time to follow a lead before things got interesting, so with my second chance at patience, I asked his name.

"Sttt…uart," he stuttered, and I knew it was a lie.

"Stttuart, *what?*" I pressed.

"Um, just Stuart," he said, nodding his head and making a gesture with his hand that indicated I should know something I did not. After a minute or so in which my blank face did not change expression, he explained, "We don't give last names. It maintains a sense of privacy."

"Oh, of course!" I said, slapping my head. "Of course I should have known! And yet I don't, so can you please tell me what the hell you are talking about? Who are *we?*"

Stttuart lowered his voice and his eyes got very wide. "Shhh. You know, the rooms?"

I shook my head and waited for him to break out the conspiracy theory that would tie in his health news of not having been injected with The Serum, after all.

"You know," he persisted, "AA? Alcoholics Anonymous?"

I continued to stare blankly at him, because I was certain this was a salad joint.

"This is where a lot of us meet our sponsors when there isn't a meeting," he explained.

Oh, okay, now I'm getting it. *Good pick, sister,* I admonished myself silently. Out loud, I said, "Where's your sponsor?"

"He left just as you were coming in."

"Well, great. Now I get you all to myself," I said sarcastically. "But I have to get to the airport now, so thanks for sharing all your news, which you did not, and continue to be well. All the best of luck to you, Stttuart." I got up, gathered my tray and started to leave.

"Aw, man, you are so judgmental, you know that? I knew I shouldn't have confided in you."

What the—?

"You did not confide in me," I answered calmly and stupidly, "and in the time that you could have, we missed our opportunity to become lifelong friends. Now, we'll never know, because I have to get to the airport. Again, congratulations on your news, and your work toward a better life. Goodbye, Muffy." I thought I had it all covered, so I tossed the salad plate into the bus bin, and took my leave.

In a bold move which caught me completely off guard, this guy followed me outside to my car and asked me if I would give him a ride home.

"You have to go that way, anyway, to get to the airport. Please? It's not that far, and I'll take my muffs off. But if you leave me to walk, they'll have to stay on, and I think we're both aware of just how much that would irritate you." He flashed a childish grin that made me laugh out loud, so I reasoned that maybe he was just a little slow in booting up the program. I motioned him into the passenger seat and started the engine. I drove him four blocks, during which he stared at me in a rather confused state, and like a child would, he investigated all the things in my cup holder: keys, quarters, my cellphone, asking questions that I never answered.

As I approached his corner, he recited a poem and then said very calmly, "I think I just came in my pants."

What?excusemeWhat? "Get out of my car immediately."

Philly Muff got out and tried to thank me through the open door, but I pulled away, ignoring him, and closed the door at the next corner.

Chapter 31

Booting Up

The visit with Squirmy was a complete bust. No interesting conversation, no cute colleagues, nothing but a waste of my time, so on the ride home, I got to thinking, *What on earth was that all about, Universe?*

I was certain that I was developing awareness in my intuition. I was following feelings and urges, and lately they had been rewarding me with at least an excellent meal. But driving to another city to waste an evening on a couple of duds?

I asked the Universe to figure it out and send me a better signal next time, and I turned up the music and flew up the turnpike home.

Two days later, I received a text from a number I didn't recognize: I have relationship issues.

It was Muffy. It took a while to put the pieces together, but apparently he'd gotten his hands on my phone in the car and dialed himself so he could add me to his contacts.

Please lose my number, I replied, and I asked the Universe once again to send me a real adventure, instead of whatever this was.

The Universe has a wicked sense of humor. It answered my plea in a series of texts from Stttuart.

I have never, ever done that before. Honest, he texted.

I deleted the texts, but he continued to send them.

I have serious relationship problems. I'm a fucking addict with codependency issues and my girlfriend broke up with me and I am weak and I can't relapse. I haven't talked to anyone since I got the news that I'm clean and could go back to work but I got fired instead. And then you talked to me.

You've got to be kidding me.

I totally understand how gross what I did was, and I'm so sorry, but I'm reaching out to you. There isn't anyone else.

You are totally, fucking kidding me, Universe. Why must you do this to me? What did I ever do to you?

I'm sorry. Please respond.

Delete. But I felt something in my gut.

I'll give my earmuffs to charity. Please.

Okay. I have no idea how this could have any relevance in my life, but this guy is not going to leave me alone, so here we go…

Why are you reaching out to me? Have you alienated everyone you know by ejaculating in front of them? One thing your mother definitely should have told you is that's a no-no. Like, not even once in a while. NO-NO.

My mother is the reason for my issues.

Of course she is, drama queen. Get your shit together and stop blaming your mom. She did the best she could.

I'm trying. She is the codependent one. She won't let me go, he insisted.

Always someone else's fault. How old are you? I meant to compare him to a child but he answered anyway.

I'll be 35. She threatens to hurt herself. Jewish Guilt is everywhere. I can't get away from her.

Try moving out of her basement, I suggested.

I have my own place. When I moved out, she didn't let me come for the holidays.

What a mess this guy is. What am I supposed to do with him? The last thing I need is a codependent addict hitching his wagon to me, fresh off my happy pills. This is not going to end well.

That sucks, I texted back. Where did you go for the holidays? The meeting rooms.

Oy.

I can't help you, I texted. I don't know what you need, and I have very little patience for your drama, so I'm not really sure that we are accomplishing anything here. Maybe your time would be better spent looking for a job.

I felt bad for this guy, but I was on my own path. I was hurting, too. I was lonely, too. I was a mess, too, in my own way. I thought for a moment that I'd like to try to help Stttuart, but I had nothing to offer, and anyway, I'd already been to the bottom of my own hole; I wasn't willing to go back down to that place for anyone, especially not a gross, disgusting stranger. Even I have limits.

I know, Miss Glitter Buns, he said. I saw your fancy snow boots and your bright funny face and I know I'm not in your league, he returned, but I don't know any other way to be than this.

I wasn't sure if that was a final signoff or a *stay-tuned-til-next-time*, so I didn't answer back and went to make dinner, silently praying that there was help out there for him. And that it wouldn't involve me.

But as the weeks went on, Stttuart sent me updates every day. Almost all of his texts mentioned the gym or "meetings." There wasn't a whole lot to chat about, but every so often I'd remind him that his unemployment wouldn't last forever, and then I admonished myself, for the only reason I entertained his texts was because I had no prospects and he gave me an excuse to yell at someone in my frustration. I was sarcastic and obnoxious, but he kept responding, so it was a convenient outlet for me.

One night, after the kids were in bed and I was ready to fall down with exhaustion, the phone buzzed with a text from Muffy.

I've never known anyone for this amount of time who only cares about what's good for me. It's kind of scary.

What?

He went on, I know you have more important things to do than yell at me about getting a job, but nobody has ever cared enough to ask me about it like you do. I think you must have fairy dust around you because I really want to try.

I didn't know how to respond. He was an absolute mess and I was abusing him further and he was *thanking* me for it.

Okay, Universe, you win. I will love this man for who he is.

I do care about you, but don't get attached to me. This is not a relationship; it's just one stranger looking out for another, got it? Now go to sleep so you can get up early and look for a job.

Chapter 32

Doing the 12-Step

Muffy was in a lot of twelve-step programs. I told him on a regular basis that I was not a therapist, nor was I trained in any way to instruct anyone on how to make their lives better. Yet, I encouraged Muffy to back off on the Meetings and Fellowship.

All these meetings, they have become a crutch, I texted him.

What do you mean? They keep me out of trouble, he would counter.

How long has it been since you were sober from everything? I asked.

Almost twelve years, almost six years, and almost three years.

And how many meetings do you go to each day?

Two or three, he responded.

Every day?" I asked him incredulously. How do you have the time?

Well, Miss Know-it-All, I haven't had a job in six months. I will surely be spiraling down that path if I have nothing to do all day.

Yeah, I suppose, I replied sympathetically, unless maybe you stop going to meetings and start going on job interviews.

That's low, he whined. I've been looking for a job. I'm applying anywhere they'll take applications.

What is it you want to do? I asked him, but he didn't know. Don't just file applications, go on interviews at places where you could be excited to work.

The concept was completely foreign. I don't have the skills they want for those jobs, he protested, not for a minute masking his fear of rejection.

Then trade in a fellowship meeting for time to learn the skills you need.

This was too much for him. And I admit, I was treading on thin ice with a fragile personality, the limits of which I was unsure. But it seemed very plain to me that he was hiding in addiction meetings—the ultimate addiction, as an excuse for not actually living his life. And since I was just starting to discover my own life, I didn't want him or anyone else to miss out on what was possible.

If you don't want to be paralyzed by addiction, how can you allow yourself to recover only to sit in a room with other addicts? Isn't that just as paralyzing?

I don't get it, he wrote back, you want me to stop going to the meetings that helped me kick my habits? You're crazy.

All I'm suggesting is that maybe you could trade in one meeting a week for two solid hours of doing something you love. You could draw, write, or learn how to cook.

I need to find a job first, he said.

But you're not doing that, either. So at least work toward smiling every day. Choose a meeting to replace with fun, and let's see where that goes. Just one meeting, just one week. Can you try that? It's an experiment.

I guess, he answered. If Miss Pixie Dust says jump, I'll jump. I'll do it if you'll come visit.

Don't do it for me, I said, it's your life. I won't be in it very long. I had to keep reminding him of this, so he wouldn't think this was a relationship. And you're not a puppy. I'm not rewarding you for doing something you need to do anyway.

The next day, he discussed the strategy with a friend, who gave him the book, *The Artist's Way* by Julia Cameron. One of the most powerful books I'd ever read, for two years I gave it out as gifts to every person I knew for every occasion. One of the very first exercises the book mandates is that the participant reader write out "morning pages," or "brain drain," to clear the mind. I was so pleased he had found it on his own, and he was ecstatic. "I'm reading this book," he told me, "and I think it might help."

I can't accurately describe the feeling I had when he told me that. It was just a book, but I knew that it would lead him on an entirely new path, away from the desperate sort of undertones his life had taken on. His unemployment checks were about to expire, and he had not a single prospect for a job, let alone a career; yet I could tell his spirit was renewed and his energy was high. My new fantasy became to see him evolve and transform his life and, just as he shed his cocoon and became a butterfly with his own wings, I would exit the scene. We then would both look fondly on our time together as a positive one, on which we would base pay-it-forward lives that would multiply out into the world.

About three weeks into *The Artist's Way* and its corresponding morning pages, and his conviction to give up two addiction meetings per week, he announced his love for writing and that his birthday was coming up. I was really happy for him and the progress he was making. He was becoming less afraid to be human, and more willing to be himself, which was a considerable improvement from the person I'd met at the salad shop, so I told him I'd come to celebrate his birthday. After much thought, I bought him six spiral notebooks and a package of pens, because twelve bucks seems like a frivolous expense when one is unemployed, yet they were clearly necessary for his well-being. I thought about how much more curious he'd become since our only meeting just a few weeks ago, and I was surprised that I really wanted to see Stttuart, and get to know who he really was.

My fragile, incapable friend was like an electric current when I arrived. He greeted me at his shabby apartment door in a towel because, he explained, he hadn't really expected me to show up. When he saw the notebooks I'd brought with me, he reacted as if I'd given him a car and a years' worth of insurance. He picked me up and hugged me for a full five minutes, not in a desperate stranglehold, but with appreciation and love pouring out of every cell in his body.

I couldn't let go of him; he was magnetic. I saw him completely differently than he had looked at the salad bar. It wasn't his hair or his face, which I hardly remembered, anyway; it was the light coming from his eyes that had made no impression on me before. There had never been a hint of physical attraction, yet I wanted to be connected to this man who was overflowing with emotion and pulling me into it. I had been wrong about Stttuart. He was beautiful, and he was powerful and human. I let him carry me to his bed, and surges of energy tore through my body over the next two hours.

We went an Italian restaurant, where one of his twelve-step friends worked and had reserved a table for him. He wanted to celebrate, not his thirty-five years, but a month of singular moments that had more impact on his life than the previous twenty had. He didn't have a job or unemployment support, he was in danger of losing his apartment, yet he had discovered the freedom to be himself, which he attested was far more valuable. "I don't know why you are interested in me at all," he said, "but I've never in my life had someone actually believe in me like you do." He quickly added, "I know I'm not supposed to expect anything, and I'm trying not to, but it's impossible not to want to succeed when I have you rooting for me."

Wow, Universe, that was a surprise. I thought of people who said: *If I can just help one person, my life will be worthwhile*...bullshit. It was intoxicating to have an effect like that on another human being. I wanted to bottle it, and I wanted to give the bottle out at bus stops and train stations, and spray it on people in department stores. It was his birthday, but it felt like Christmas to me.

Soon after our visit, I noticed the texting wasn't quite as frequent. Once or twice during the day, I'd teasingly ask him if he was rocking himself in a corner waiting for me to come back, and an hour or two later, I'd get a text that said, Busy day or writing a lot. It finally dawned on me that he had found his inspiration and didn't need me to field his made-up drama texts anymore.

I had wondered briefly, after that whole display on his birthday, whether he would think we had a relationship; and floored by the distinct awareness that once again, I had experienced a level of love so epic—so sincere and full—and yet I had no attachment to it. I said a prayer of thanks for that magical evening we shared; and I released myself from any further expectation. I meditated on the fact that it had always been my intention to be *worth* undying gratitude from Muffy and all the others; but that I wouldn't need to have it broadcast for my ego's benefit. That we both acknowledged and knew that our time together was producing magic was enough to fill me while I was schlepping through my daily duties. Still, my ego was pretty happy.

Another few days went by, and he texted that he had been waiting to tell me that he got a job. He wasn't proud of it, but a friend had given him the name of a seedy hotel that needed housekeeping. It was late at night, and the kids were asleep, so I called him, to hear his voice, and to congratulate him.

"Don't get excited," he said, his own voice an octave higher. "It's pretty nasty stuff."

I didn't care. "I want to hear all about it," I urged, and he began to tell me how he was learning what cleans up cum stains and blood.

I laughed. "Sounds like quite a filling station for your creative writing ideas. Do you have to wear a Hazmat suit?"

"No, nothing like that, but it is pretty gross," he replied. Then he added, "and you're the only one in the world that would think this was a cool job. I never thought about it like that. You're always so positive."

"It's a perfect job," I exclaimed, truly thrilled for him. "Lots of time for your imagination to wander to your writing and think up great stories. And you get paid to do it, what's better than that?"

There was silence on the line for a minute or two, and I listened to him breathe. "You make me feel like a superhero," he said finally.

"You are a superhero," I said quietly. "You just don't know it yet."

Chapter 33

Superhero School

With Muffy well on his way toward a brighter future, which would soon turn into an even better job driving a truck and making deliveries in the countryside, accompanied by photography classes as a result of his awe of the nature he drove through every day, it finally dawned on me that what he appreciated most about me was something I could apply at home.

There wasn't any need to scream at the kids for forgetting to put shoes away or for not brushing their teeth or for forgetting their homework. *Start treating them like superheroes* I told myself, and I began to think about the ways that I had encouraged Muffy, himself an overgrown child, and I began to look for ways to bring that into my own world.

It seemed the thing he had responded to most had been that I never threatened to leave, yet there was always the understanding that I wouldn't be there forever; and so I began to shift my schedule so that the kids would have as few unnecessary hours as possible with Grandma Sitter. That left me time for myself, but still allowed me to have special, concentrated time with each child to help them develop their individual interests. Muffy also was happy to take on responsibility for himself, as long as he wouldn't be ridiculed for it; and so I began to praise the kids for creativity and make them responsible for things. When my youngest stacked the dishwasher with the cereal bowls right-side up, still filled with oatmeal and milk and sloshing all over, I didn't explain anything. I let the machine run, and when the bowls came out as dirty as they went in, I got the kids together to figure out how to get a better result.

It was fascinating. I even experimented with them the day I had a headache that wouldn't quit. I called them into my room one Wednesday morning and told them I simply couldn't stand up, and did they think they could get themselves off to school? I texted a neighbor to be on the lookout for them, listened for the door to slam, and went down to find the lunchboxes gone and peanut butter and bologna next to the bread wrapper haphazardly twisted closed on the counter, grapes and Goldfish lying next to plastic lunch containers with mismatched lids. I knew they had tried all the possible combinations, and that they had been successful enough to produce a midday meal. One small step for mankind!

I tried it at bedtime: the bathroom was flooded, but their hair smelled of shampoo, and their mouths of mint. I told them they were so grown up to get themselves ready all by themselves, and could they try to tackle cleaning the bathroom after school the next day? Sure enough, all the towels were hung to dry, no lumps of Colgate were found in the basin, and the wastebasket was filled with Lysol wipes. They couldn't wait to show me.

It wasn't like suddenly they began cleaning the bathroom without being asked. I still had to remind them and—on occasion—scream in frustration; we're all human. But now that I knew it was in them…what other superpowers might I have been overlooking? What superpowers might I find within myself? My eyes were wide with the anticipation of each new possibility.

My chance encounter at the salad café wasn't random at all, of course. I had trusted in that, but the bigger picture had been amazing for me to witness. I learned to be a better parent by allowing myself to go on an adventure with someone my own parents might have warned me about. We are all teachers, we are all students, and we don't get to decide which one we will be in a given situation.

Now there's a sobering thought.

Chapter 34

Yugo, I Go

Thanks to several months of experimenting with willing participants, my default had become a state of love, adventure, possibility, and opportunity. Granted, life was a series of challenges to that mantra, but I had a genuine appreciation for my life and the people in it. On a beautiful September day, I took a drive to visit a childhood friend who lived in Westchester County, north of New York City, which meant a drive over the magnificent George Washington Bridge. That day, there happened to be a huge traffic jam on the interstate leading to it.

As I watched agitated drivers come to a screeching halt from their cruise speed, then drive *over the median* in aggressive attempts to circumvent the impending doom of their commute, I decided there were two ways to go about it: freak out and follow suit, or take a few deep breaths and let my friend know I'd be a bit later than I'd planned. I chose the latter, and looked up through the sunroof to see a beautiful blue sky, grateful for the happy circumstance of extra time to myself with my great new playlist filling my ears. I closed my eyes for a moment, smiled, and felt the warm sun on my face…along with the slight sting of a wadded up piece of coffee-stained paper that bounced off my forehead.

I couldn't believe that people still littered in this day and age; and since weird stuff like this happened to me a lot, I unwadded the wad, and sure enough, there was a phone number written on it.

I looked around, and about three lanes over, I saw a moving van with four sweaty guys stuffed into the cab, smiling and waving furiously at me. I looked back down at the paper and dialed the number. I watched as one of the guys in the middle picked up and, looking back at me, screamed into the phone, "I can't believe it!" as if he'd just won concert tickets on the Morning Zoo.

"Hello," I replied, trying to match the excitement in his voice. "What can I do for you?"

"Your smile," he said, "ees like I can feel zee energy of you."

I laughed and asked him why he felt the need to bean me with a paper ball.

"You were next to me all zee way back zare. I can't let you get away for your smile."

"Where are you from?" I asked.

"Ees leetle country was Yugoslavia."

"Okay," I replied, mentally adjusting my verbal decoding skills. I had a feeling he was going to be a chatterbox.

"What is your name, princess of zee smiles and zee energies? Oh, I can feel it big, zee energies!"

"What is your name?" I asked loudly, as a foreign traveler might.

"Princess," he said. "You are a princess to me, your Matthew."

Just like that, on the GW Bridge on a warm, sunny day, I became a princess with a loyal subject. Not bad for traffic hell that others would call the worst part of their day. How lovely it felt to have the new, improved me be recognized literally, for the energy I was sending out into the world that day! I mean, who does that? Stops you in traffic to compliment your energy?

I continued to chat with Matthew until I just couldn't understand any more of his extended vocabulary. When the time came to finally end our conversation, he pleaded, "Oh, princess, please do not forget your Matthew. I must see you again!"

I giggled and hung up, but sure enough, Matthew texted me throughout the day, with each stop he made delivering furniture, to give me zee update zat I am a princess.

It continued on, every other day or so until the holidays. I asked him if he had any plans to go home to Yugoslavia for Christmas.

No, I stay and wait for my princess to come, he texted.

It had to be getting old on his end, but he just kept keeping it up. Finally, over Christmas break, when X had the kids and I had a few days to myself, I penciled him in. It was a long way to go, but I couldn't let this continue. This guy invested a lot of time in these texts, and it was time to improve his English. And maybe check out his moving man's body.

Oh, what dream is come true! he texted.

We made plans to meet for dinner, and since he did not have a car, I told him I would pick him up. I set out with plenty of time for holiday bridge traffic, and began my journey to Matthew's neighborhood in the Bronx. I let Kali know where I was headed, but I was unconcerned; this sweet, foreign soul seemed incapable of harm. Anyway, it was Christmastime, and I was full of joy, so what the hell, *here we go…*

I turned my car carefully onto his alley-wide block, looking for the address of his building. Although he had sent a text picture of himself weeks ago, I had long since forgotten what he looked like. I needn't have worried; I couldn't miss him this time. There he stood, at the entrance to his apartment house, smiling with every tooth visible, lit up like a Christmas tree and holding an enormous teddy bear, the kind you see hanging high over the Atlantic City boardwalk, with a big red ribbon wrapped around its neck, and balancing one of those 700-piece candy hearts that guys who cheat bring to their wives on Valentine's Day. I'm guessing he spent a week's paycheck on that display of affection.

"Princess," he said, pushing the bear toward me, beaming. "This for you, to keep you warm if I cannot."

I couldn't help but smile. "And this," I motioned to the velvet heart-shaped box, "Are you trying to induce diabetic shock?"

He stared at me blankly, then said somewhat predictably, "Nothing is sweet like my princess. I try to equal as much, but this is as big as I could find."

We buckled the bear into the backseat, the giant candy-filled heart taking up the seat next to it, and headed to dinner. Matthew made a reservation at a very large, family-style Italian restaurant. We were shown to our table, where I had to explain that it was unacceptable for both of us to sit on the same side of the booth.

"I want to be close with you," he said. "I want never to let you away from near my arms."

"That's very flattering…and creepy," I replied. Then a little softer, I tried, "I prefer to look at your smile."

Boy was I wrong. His smile did not quit, not for one second out of the entire evening at that table. I needed sunglasses. He just kept smiling and smiling, bigger and bigger. I wondered how anyone had the cheek muscles for it, and it was a little bit uncomfortable, frankly.

We managed to have a conversation in broken English, and I did a lot of pantomiming and correcting his gross misuse of the language, but all in all, it was an informative conversation about where he was from, where he currently lived, what he hoped to be, and that I was his princess.

"You smile," he said, himself giddy with his wide grin, "you smile and is like my whole world is alive, is like zee sun is looking only at me." He had some smooth lines, for a guy with no command of the language.

"Yes, but do you have family back in Yugoslavia?"

"And I cannot believe, you are here now with me."

"How long have you been working with this moving company?"

"Is good job, I like, and then I see your text and I am smiling."

"Uh-huh, and do you know how to cook?"

"I cook ze steak and I will cook anything my princess to chew."

This was all very fine and good for my completely inflated ego, but we had been at it for two hours and well, it was starting to sound a little insincere.

No, actually, it was starting to sound sad. For four months, this beautiful man sitting across the table from me had texted all the things that most guys text me—how they would like to meet, and asking if I would just send one picture? They promised not to share it with anyone—but this guy had really meant it. He'd waited all this time, professed his devotion to me, went to work and came home and waited for me to come. And I had showed up, looking for a good time, an adventurous night out, and he was *devoted* to me. How was I supposed to take advantage of that?

Most of my text boyfriends looked for a little fun, a little bit of a story to tell the guys at work. And since I kind of think like a guy in most cases, especially the ones where there would be no harm in a good time, I was usually happy to oblige. Fun is fun. But this one was different. Matthew was planning on taking me to meet his parents, so sure that this was not just love at first sight, but *true* love at first sight. That, I was simply not expecting.

I asked him if I could pay for dinner, hoping to alleviate a little bit of the guilt of just wanting to roll around with a manual laborer, but he was too excited to let me.

We retrieved the car from the valet and I drove him home. He eagerly directed me to a parking lot near his apartment, but as soon as I realized he wanted me to come upstairs with him, I knew I had to get out of there. How could I be sure there wasn't a Yugolsavian clergyman waiting for us? He was so wound up that he might chop me to bits and put me in the freezer just to keep me near him.

"I'm not coming up with you," I said assertively.

"Princess, I understand you are busy and not much time for your Matthew. I will do what you say."

That was easy. "Thank you for understanding," I added for good karma.

"But Princess," he went on, "I am here, always I wait for you. I mean for to be real, this feelings I have for you. Do not let such much time go on as before I see you."

"I cannot promise anything, and I am not responsible to be your happy," I said firmly to him, just to make sure he understood. "I'm going now."

"Okay, my princess. I wait again for you."

"No, don't wait."

"You see. I wait til time is always."

"I may not come at all."

"You are zee light of zee sun."

"Get out of the car." It was now so completely ridiculous that I had no choice but to be mean.

He got out of the car and blew me a kiss as he skipped back into his building, not knowing it would be the first, last, and only time we would meet. Because there's a responsibility that comes with love. He was willing to give himself unconditionally to me, based on a smile, and an exchange of energy that was so forceful it could have been magic; yet I was unwilling to allow for the possibility and ante up the real deal in return. I wasn't prepared for that kind of obligation.

Unable to see around my huge ego that was inflated every time he told me that the light of my smile dwarfed that of the sun, I missed out on what might have been a very human connection, a chance to connect with someone so unlike me that I may have learned a thing or two about the simplicity of Love, Yugoslavian-style.

But then, I could have been found years later in the freezer, too.

Chapter 35

Man, Manifested

continued to ride high with my adventures and experiments. I loved that I was learning so much about men to whom I previously would never have given the time of day; and I became more full of myself as they multiplied and openly expressed the good I'd brought into their lives. There were executives, students, public servants, service reps, CEOs, manual laborers, artists, foreigners, fishmongers—the list went on from people I met in airports, on highways, at farmer's markets, sporting events, restaurants, repair shops, the beach—and that list went on as well.

I was fascinated by the way they swooped in and out of my life, leaving little golden bits of love behind for me, and even a few marriage proposals. In fact, that's how the powerful cycle of love through giving and receiving, became a selfish quest of the power within me to see what else I could conquer, and a lesson in humility—and still, everything happened for a reason.

I had done my share of traveling for a while, so I set to making a cozy home for the winter. The kids and I started baking cookies and decorating for the holidays, and I was appreciating all of the homemaking tasks that I had so abhorred while they were toddlers. I had been feeling healthy, and my heart was feeling full enough that I asked X to join us for Thanksgiving and Christmas, so that the kids wouldn't have to keep track of the every-other-holiday dread. He agreed, and that seemed to lift the spirits of everyone.

It had been a couple of months, and well into the season that "Coach" had been volunteering on my son's football team, when I saw him at school one day.

"Love that kid of yours," he said. "He's a real fighter. I'd like to recruit him for wrestling. What do you think?"

Wrestling—the kind with rules, anyway—was not a popular sport in our house, but I knew my son liked this guy, and with Dad at a different address, I was always on the lookout for positive everyday male role models, so I told him I'd make the suggestion, but no guarantees.

"Well, if you have any questions, here's my cell number..."

Uh oh.

"I'm not sure you want to give me that. You could be asking for trouble," I said, with a mischievous smile.

"I like trouble," he winked. "Don't say it if you don't mean it," and he turned and walked away, waving over his shoulder.

At this point in other realms of my experiments, I had been playing with the idea of manifestation, and at this point, it was time to take on my white-collar, upper-middle class neighborhood. I thought it might be cool to rustle up a manly-man in jeans and a pickup truck, in contrast to the men in impeccable Armani suits in Audis that barely slowed down as they unlocked the doors for their kids to spill out onto the sidewalk at the school drop-off. Now here he was, out of nowhere, complete with work boots, climbing into the king cab of his big, shiny working-guy's testosterone mobile. I had never noticed him or it before, in all these weeks of football practices.

Damn it all.

What time is the tryout? I texted.

6 p.m. Hope to see ya there.

After the wrestling exhibition practice, to which I took my kids, and which predictably they hated, Coach pulled me aside.

"It finally hit me," he said. "You're the one my wife keeps telling me I should meet."

"Why? I asked, "Do I know her?"

"She said you met at a party. Apparently we have a lot in common."

I scanned my memory and landed upon a woman I met at a baby shower some months back. As we chatted, she'd suddenly exclaimed, "You should meet my husband. You two would get along great."

"That's not something you hear very often," I'd said.

"I'm serious," she'd insisted. "You have so much in common, and I sure as hell don't know what to do with him." She had laughed and the momma-to-be had laughed, and the whole room had laughed, and everyone there seemed to be in on the joke that I didn't get.

"Okay," I shrugged, "but you're the one who suggested it."

I never got her name.

"Oh!" I exclaimed, concluding the memory and coming back into the present conversation. "You and I share a birthday! But I can't remember what else we're supposed to bond over."

"Well," he said, "*my* birthday is coming up. Wanna have lunch and find out?"

Chapter 36

Birthday Date

Over lunch in a neighborhood café, Coach presented me with a tiny, doll-sized tool kit.

"Happy birthday. I just had a feeling you might like this." A strange gift for sure, but he had no way of knowing, at this, our first meeting off school property, that I had just lost one that I'd kept with me for years, to airport security. Immediately, my intuitive antennae went up.

We ordered lunch, and chatted for about an hour, confirming that his wife had been right; lots in common, easy familiarity. Coach was charming and I liked his wry sense of humor, and there was a realness to his character that I sensed immediately. As we walked out to the sunlight of the midday, he leaned in for the obligatory hug.

"Thanks for meeting me. That was the best lunch I've had in a long time." Then, as he pulled away, he stopped inches from my face. "Hey, do you have time for a walk?"

"Sure," I said, "what's up?"

As we walked around the block, Coach got right to the point.

"I'm not the world's greatest husband," he said. "I've got a real hard time going home at night."

"Why are you telling me this?" I said, treading lightly with my new friend.

"I can't shake it," he said. "My wife and I've had some—what do they call it, *issues?*—and I can't let them go. I'm really afraid that I'm taking my problems with her out on our daughters. I can't help it; they look just like her…" His voice trailed off, and his eyes seemed to follow it off in the distance, and I was stuck between confused and cocky. Was this a plea for a friend, or for an affair?

It didn't matter, either way. In my ego-bloat, fresh off some pretty stunning victories, I was willing to fix him, whatever it meant. The Universe sent him, oddly enough, via his wife, so…*here we go!*

"I'm not sure how I can help, but you've got my number if you need me," I offered.

He looked at me with the face of a sweet little boy. "Do you mean that?'

"Of course. I never say things I don't mean."

"I can't take it anymore. I'm ready to leave her."

"Oh, I don't think you mean that. What makes you think you have no responsibility for your…*issues?*"

"That's just it. I know it's not her fault, but every time I look at her, I just get angry. I can't forgive her."

"Maybe you need to forgive yourself first," I offered.

"What the hell does that mean?" he asked with a contorted face, as if I had just started speaking Japanese.

"Listen, Ace, I'm a little light on the facts here, but what I'm getting is that you are struggling with something big, and if it's that big, it's not fair for you to make her carry it all by herself. Which means you can't, either, and I can tell from your face that you've already tried to take on that load and dropped it. So don't just stand around cursing that it's too heavy. Forgive yourself for your lack of strength and ask for help."

"What planet are you from?" he asked.

I giggled. "I tend to get a little out there," I said, "but it just seemed obvious."

He shook his head as if to snap out of what he'd just heard.

"Anyway, just think about it and get back to me," I said.

"Oh, I will, thanks," he said thoughtfully. "Hey, that only saying what you mean? Does that go for the 'trouble' thing, too?" he asked with a grin, immediately lightening up and diffusing the heaviness that hung in the air.

"You have no idea. I would seriously think twice about that one if I were you," I admonished him, and he threw back his head and guffawed, and hugged me goodbye again.

"Okay, killer," he said. "I'll take you at your word. See ya later."

Chapter 37

Coaching Coach

t was a nice day, my birthday. Lunch with my new friend, Coach; chocolate chip pancakes with smiley faces that the kids made for dinner; and all was right in my world.

Later, Coach sent me a text: Who do I ask for help? Only one I can think of is God, and I'm mad at Him, too.

I responded: If your kids are mad at you and they still need their shoes tied, who do they ask to tie them?

My wife.

Then go ask her.

Coach began to send me texts every day after school.

Hey killer, I liked your boots today, he'd text.

Talk to your wife or I'll kick your ass with 'em.

Promise?

Or,

It's raining pretty hard out there. Wanna carpool? he'd ask.

Thanks, but puddle-splashing is a lost art.

You're nuts.

It wasn't long before the evening texts would arrive.

Hey killer, I didn't see you at school today. Where were you?

I wasn't sure if he was looking for his own adventure, or if he was really avoiding some deep pain, but I knew that I wasn't going to initiate an affair. Although I I knew I wouldn't mind spending some time with him, it felt pretty close to home.

Even as I knew he would seek me out, this time I would be innocent. After all, I'd manifested him and he'd dropped in my lap, complete with an endorsement from the wife. But if his *issues* were easily fixed, I really didn't want to get involved at all, other than to listen. I asked him what was really going on at home.

It's too much to text.

Then why are you texting me when your wife is right there? Talk to her.

It's complicated.

Nothing is complicated.

Can you meet me tomorrow?

People speak in different languages. Some use sarcasm, or innuendo, self-deprecation, body language; and as one of my, shall we say, *intuitive gifts*, I could see through most of it pretty quickly. Coach was full of raw, physical angst, and he needed space for his uniquely angry expression. I wasn't ashamed to offer to hold that space for him—not because I wanted to have an affair with a married father who lived down the block—because I certainly knew we could be getting on a wild ride to a dark place. But because even then, with all my feathers puffed up, waiting to be The Answer, I knew that nobody could hear this guy the way I could, the way he knew that I understood his specific dialect. I had already been to the dark place. I wasn't going back there, but I was willing to hand him a flashlight. And here he was in front of me, asking for batteries.

I knew that it was a crazy choice to get involved with him, but I also wanted to see how brave I really was, match his devil-may-care attitude; still, I asked him again and again, *Do you want this kind of trouble?* His pain was impossible to ignore. He didn't care. Either way, from where he stood, his marriage didn't stand a chance.

For my part, I was getting restless. In our small, uptight town of two cars, two kids, two cats, and a dog at the end of every manicured lawn, I was rebelling against the perfect life that I was "stuck" with. I laughed as I thought of the irony of how I'd worked to create it, only to want so acutely to destroy it. I was already the subject of some great gossip (the *divorcees* always are); and now that I had taken charge of myself enough to be useful to others through some big stuff, I was ready to take on the whole damn town, and show them *what this little hussy can do!*

But in all my wanting to be wanted, I genuinely intended to help Coach. I knew from the beginning that whatever was about to happen, and no matter what he said about his marriage being over, the point of our meeting through the strangest of circumstances was to get him to come to grips with his family situation and go back to his wife in a better state. I was ready for some fun along the way, but at the end of the ride, I knew I was getting off, and he was going home. Of this, I was certain.

I met him that Friday evening at his friend's office, several miles outside of town. His anger and frustration were apparent from the moment he kissed me, hard and authoritatively, and with no pretense, we segued right to sex, raw and unemotional.

"You have got to be the hottest mom in town," he said when he was done.

"Super," I said, unimpressed. "You reeled in the big one. Now what was that all about?"

Finally, his emotions began to flow, and Coach confirmed what I'd felt all along; that he was a brilliant man in search of answers to questions he didn't know how to ask. He was quoting literature, trying to put into words the anguish he felt, and find the actions that would let him escape it. He was losing his family and he didn't know if he wanted to save it.

"How is this happening? How ironic is it that I've landed here with you in my arms, not because I'm the cat's pajamas, but because you are trying to help a man who can't be helped?"

"Who says you can't be helped?" I asked, as we got dressed, unconcerned that this was not a romantic date, but an after-hours mission of sorts.

I loved the contrast between brain and brawn in him. He was rough around the edges, and still his heart was true. But Coach gave me a lot of power. I was the one, in his eyes, that had it all together, and he thought he could get his own power back through being with me, like it was some kind of STD, not realizing it was just another distraction from the *issues*. He was intelligent enough to know that he needed a new life or a new perspective, but with his family to support, the former wasn't an option, so we spent a lot of time on the latter.

"Look," I said, "I'm tired of hearing about how much you hate your wife. You're not leaving her, or else you already would have. She is the mother of your children, so she can't be *all* bad. Can you at least concede that?"

"She tricked me into marriage by getting pregnant."

"Oh geez, what are you, twelve? If you're that stupid and irresponsible, then you deserve what you got. And you got cool little people out of it, so let's try to think of it in a better light, shall we?"

"What's your idea of better light, *Oh, wise swami?*"

"Love," I said simply.

"Yeah, yeah. Love," he said dismissively.

"Love," I said again, staring him down. "Your children represent love. They couldn't have been born without it."

Coach got quiet and then his face turned soft, sad, old.

"She tricked me with the one that didn't make it. A boy. I loved her then."

I waited for him to go on.

"I was going to have a son. I was so happy. I loved her then. We got married, and she lost him. After that, only girls."

I was stunned. And furious. "*This* is your issue?" I roared. "That you have healthy girls, but no boys?"

"She lost him. I know it's not logical. I know it's not her fault. But I'll never get over that. I tried, but I can't, we can't…"

Against my instinct, I held him while he tried to regain his composure. I wanted to punch him. I wanted to pick up his head and spin it around like they do in cartoons, and I wanted to take back this whole stupid idea of being with him.

And then, I remembered the one I'd lost.

"Love is the only thing that can heal this," I said quietly.

"I gotta go," he said, breaking the silence as he grabbed his coat. "Thanks for listening. Thanks for understanding." And he held the door for me wordlessly, walked me to my car, and looking away while he half-assed a one-arm hug, said, "I'll see ya later."

Chapter 38:

It Ain't Over
'Til It's Over

As expected, I didn't hear from him over the weekend. Experience has taught me that when you hit someone with something you think they need to hear but aren't ready for, it takes a while to process while they're pissed off at you. I hadn't discounted the fact that he had a family and two days' worth of kids' soccer, either. By Sunday night, he was back, like nothing ever happened. I love this genetic defect—or genius—in men, the ability to recalibrate without explanation.

Hey, killer, how was your weekend?

Perfect. Yours?

Your ass is perfect. Especially in those jeans you wore on Friday.

Ah, yes. Reduced to the physical. One step forward, two steps back. It was nice that he noticed, though. As long as we were changing gears, I would have a little fun, too.

If you like them so much, why'd ya take them off?

Wanted to see if it lived up to the hype. Then, Totally did.

I giggled to myself and said goodnight. I had other texts waiting for replies, and he didn't seem to need me.

The next morning, Coach texted me very early. Where do I find love in a heart that's already hardened over?

Ask God's wife. Then, And listen for the answer.

Okay, *Swami.* Will it come through the car radio, or do I have to set up a special antenna?

Go to work, Ace.

The days became routine, each morning an early text about accessing love, and each afternoon a comment about my boots or my jeans. I never texted him because I didn't want to risk him answering a text while he was trying to fix his relationship, which he was, in his own way.

I loved the attention I was getting as the high priestess, the way he always deferred to me as if I knew some ancient secret. I felt like, by virtue of his searching, I *did* have some ancient secret; it only needed to be uncovered. And laying himself before me only made me want to help him more, to prove that I was worthy of his attention, not just a wanton dalliance. I was really connecting with and learning so much about his very complex soul, and shifting from primal to intellectual to spiritual had us both wading through emotions so intense they could have been measured on the Richter scale. I was fascinated by the power we were willing to give each other with such deep trust that nobody else would understand, yet it was only ever meant to be a small, measured opening in which to work on matters of interest only to us.

Early morning: *Swami,* is there an angel of love? I've been praying to the Virgin Mary, but I don't seem to be getting anywhere.

Try Mary Magdalene. She's my go-to for forgiveness, and love is in forgiveness.

Will do. See ya later. Wear that scarf again. It's hot.

Evening: Night, killer. Thanks for listening, as always.

And so it would go. There were evenings when we'd meet to run errands together and maybe toss in a quickie, always fun and sneaky, but I was convinced that it was all part of the process of softening Coach's heart. I saw it as the end justifying the means, like a cardiac surgeon who breaks open a heart in order to save it, or a pregnant belly that must be cut in order to bring the little life inside to breathe—counter-productive during the process, yet after the procedure, there would be great healing. I saw it as the radical action that would lead to the breakthrough.

A couple of weeks went by.

Early morning: Mornin, *Swami*. Any idea who Kwan Yin is?

She's the goddess of compassion. Why do you ask?

My wife has a statue of her on the dresser. I just asked her about it and she said that's who it was, but she wasn't exactly sweet about it. You're sweet about it.

That was the day I asked Coach to meet me at the pizza place for lunch. If there's one thing I love, it's a clear sign from the Universe.

"I think it's time," I said, when he arrived.

"Time for what?" he asked, raising his eyebrows.

"How long has Kwan Yin been on the dresser?"

He hesitated, so I answered for him.

"How 'bout say, since just after you lost your son."

"How did you know…?"

"Kwan Yin is the one-size-fits-all symbol for love, compassion, and forgiveness."

He looked at me wide-eyed, like the little boy I saw on our birthday.

"And you just noticed her today. It's a clear sign that it's time to forgive your wife, the baby, God, and yourself. You're ready."

All in all, the affair lasted a month, give or take a week. He had been heard, he'd released his anger and found forgiveness, and I'd had a profoundly self-absorbing blast helping him to do so. I found that more than the secret sex and getting away with it, I had mostly enjoyed being the conduit for the transformation that had taken place within him. It was pretty heady stuff, thinking that I had "fixed" him by my creative "therapy." Sex had turned out to be the tool that served us both in the process.

We were just wrapping up our mission together when I got the phone call. I'm not sure whether I was expecting it or not.

"It's not about you," I said, softly but defiantly.

"What do you mean, it's not about me?" his wife demanded. "That's my husband you've been whoring around with, and that makes it *all* about me."

I'm human, and I hated to be caught, and I was high on our results, and I was *right*. I wanted to ask her if she had noticed something was wrong before *he or I* did something, or remind her that *she* encouraged us to meet, but the truth was, she was scared, and she needed to have her expression of anger be heard, too.

So instead, I responded that their relationship was none of my business, and suggested that her attention might be better spent talking to him.

I said, "I wish you both the very best," and I meant it.

A few minutes later, my phone buzzed with a text from Coach: Don't text me anymore.

I knew that they were her words, but I never spoke to nor texted either of them again.

In my own righteousness, I was astounded that people believed that because they had married someone, then by law, they owned that person; that they had actually been deeded that human being, and therefore had every right to violate any confidence regarding that person of which they were not a part. I understood that conventional wisdom said that two people joined in matrimony were not to be pulled asunder, but I had yet to witness two people who needed no one else in their lives.

My time spent with Coach had been precious. Although we never fell in love, and I'd been told that I was a whore and a home wrecker, I believed that Coach and I were put in a very specific place and time to learn lessons about love that served us both. The circumstances in which we found ourselves ranged from inexplicable to magical, but the results were miraculous.

Coach and his family moved to the town they had talked about, in better days, having gained the one thing that had eluded him all his life: a son, born exactly nine months after we parted; and I have gained a perspective on judgment that has served me every single day since. I am grateful to Coach, for his boldness in reaching out to me (inexplicable) and his vulnerability (magical); to his wife, for both insisting on our meeting (inexplicable) and forcing its end (magical); and to the Universe, for all of the incredible circumstances that have allowed me to be a witness to human nature, in the search for the light within each of us, and the love that's screaming to get out of us.

I was aware that I'd committed an adulterous act, and I wasn't exactly proud of that; but I wasn't ashamed, either. Underneath it all, I believed that love had the last word, and that love continued to grow where it was once dormant. All it needed was a little encouragement, a little interpretation, and a willing guinea pig. I don't know if the end justified the means, but having seen Coach in extreme states of both despair and joy, I'll take joy any day of the week.

Chapter 39

Bravely into the Fog

The spring arrived, and with it an opportunity to visit Paul Bunyan at his tiny, new studio apartment in Chicago. I had a special spot in my heart for that city, so I planned a night at a hotel in addition to our agreed-upon 24 hours, with the intention of seeing what the Universe put in front of me.

As was becoming standard operating procedure, I met a man at the airport while waiting for my flight. He was so busy on his iPhone in the airport bar that I made it my mission to get him to take three consecutive bites of his lunch without looking at it.

He said, "Tell ya what, Darlin. You get me offa this thing for good, and I'll marry you and we can retire to Tahiti. But 'til then, I gotta make a living."

We got to chatting and he taught me to use the more precise emotions of the emoji keyboard on my phone, and I sent him a text-blown kiss as my flight departed a short while later.

Paul Bunyan and I had a lovely time. While the romance had been dialed down quite a bit, we spent the day like an old couple, or perhaps best friends from childhood, holding hands and taking in the city with an easy pace that suggested we'd known each other forever. We slept comfortably together in his bed after a night of genuine intimacy, and when our time together was complete, we said goodbye easily, both knowing that we had just seen each other for the last time; and yet we were never more than a text away if a lifeline was needed.

I cherished this part of my heart that was able to let go lovingly and fully; *easy-come-easy-go* was a foreign concept in matters of the heart for most people, and I fully appreciated that anyone I've ever loved could be set free, and yet could still remain in my heart forever.

It's a practice; I was certainly not the only woman in the world that had never had a bad breakup or a rocky relationship, and even then, when they ended, it was never easy. But over time, I'd come to believe that it's the *love,* not the *someone,* that mattered, so I would let go *just to see* if I could console myself with the faith that as long as I'd fully loved, the next one would be even better. This I believed as surely as night followed day, and the post-game analysis was clear. Although I was still processing the end of the affair with Coach, and remnants of X that were still floating around, Paul Bunyan was a perfectly timed, joyfully fun, beautiful soul to confirm that newly developed faith.

The next night in my uber-urban hotel, there was a party in the lobby populated by models and the men who want to sleep with them. I was tired, but I was curious to see if it was fueled by the same kind of insecurities that I had encountered years ago when I had moved here to model. From a different perspective, no longer based on the fear of rejection, I enjoyed the evening, meeting the fabulous and the wannabes, and then I headed upstairs, alone. I got ready for bed and checked my phone. The man from the airport had sent me a heart emoji.

Thank you for taking my head out of my ass. The view was much better, he wrote, then amended it to say, and I apologize for my language just now. I don't often text beautiful women like you. He followed with emojis of hearts and flowers.

He was a sweet texter, but I let him know I was on a weekend journey, so he left me alone for the most part. He texted that he would have liked to join me, and that he was thinking of me more than he could help.

The next morning, I took a walk out toward Lake Michigan. Back when I'd lived here, I never did that, somehow thinking it was the private domain of the folks who lived in the high-rise buildings along Lakeshore Drive. Rather, I had stayed on my end of town, near the Chicago River, and walked the streets of the city instead.

This time, I followed the concrete path out into the waters of the lake, as the fog came in at a rapid pace. I wasn't sure what was leading me to walk so far in those conditions, but once I began, it was impossible to turn back. There was something inside me that was pulling me forward, refusing to let me turn around until I came to the end of wherever the path was taking me. The fog was getting more dense, and the concrete was getting more narrow as I continued, and the people I had seen earlier had disappeared. I was alone.

Just as I had been alone all those years ago when I lived in this cold, windy city. Right up until the day before Mom died. Just a wannabe like the people in the hotel, the beautiful parts of the city off limits, and just when I couldn't take it anymore, I go home and Mom dies. Rejected from every angle. And here I am again, with the scab of my dead marriage and the fresh wound of another soulmate, gone.

The thoughts were making me shake with every step. I thought I loved the city; but suddenly I knew I was there to heal the pain it had inflicted upon me.

I was unsteady on my feet, crying at the memories, so perfectly enshrouded in the thick fog of the morning. I was empty and I was hungry. I was hungry for answers, I was hungry for love. I needed to be nourished. Where was I on this journey? I believed so firmly in certain things; yet I was so uncertain still. Why am I here?

The path was all crumbled now, so narrow that in the fog I thought I should surely lose my balance. Was I on the yellow brick road or the path to oblivion? I stopped and steadied myself, took out my cellphone and turned on the GPS locator. I gasped as I looked at the map; it showed a tiny dot—me—at the end of a thin line, surrounded by water on the entire screen. I was practically in the middle of Lake Michigan, on the tiny tip of a concrete barrier! Another few steps, a gust of wind, and...

I held my breath, and turned slowly around to see if I could retrace my steps through the clouds. Just then, a figure came out of the smoke, a beautiful, petite blond wearing a sports bra with an iPod clipped to it, bounding lightly toward me. She passed me gingerly, touched the ground, and whirled around to go back to where she came from, smiling as she jogged, and disappeared back into the ether. In an instant, I had gone from scared and lonely to confused and curious, and I followed her lead back to the mainland, trying to find the significance of my disorientation in the fog, compared to the jogger's complete assertiveness of knowing exactly where she was and where she was going.

Perspective! Focus! Clarity! I shouted to myself. I wasn't lost; I was letting go of the old ways I had been traveling through life. *What a metaphor*: shedding the heavy, crumbling concrete of my old, unclear ways to make way for a new path. Yet, without clearly knowing which hunger I needed to satisfy, I would be lost forever on a gangplank in the mist; maybe if I could just get focused on where I wanted to go, the clear path would emerge. *It's all about trust and clarity and perspective.* And in that strangely orchestrated instant, I knew that I would trust unconditionally in the love of the Universe, and my fear of the past repeating would release itself.

I made my way back much more quickly than I had left, and followed the reappearing crowd out of the fog, into the daylight, all the way to the corner of civilization. I crossed with the light, resolving to feed my soul whatever it needed. There, on the other side of the street was a pancake house. And a text from my new friend from the airport on my phone. Life, *my life*, was full indeed.

I texted Kali: Pancakes and possibilities.

Chapter 40

Parkway Dad

At this point, I could scarcely get into my car without a new text boyfriend logged into my phone by the time I got out of it. Every red light, every merging lane, every toll booth seemed to bring with it a new gentleman with a cellphone who wanted to get to know mine.

So it came as no surprise to me that, after signing the papers for the beach house I had just manifested, I found myself sitting in heavy traffic on the parkway, inching along next to a man in a white pickup truck wearing aviator sunglasses, nodding and playing with the dangly thing hanging from his rear-view mirror, occasionally looking over and smiling at me.

When I noticed the sticker of a hockey goalie on the back of his truck, I felt a tingle of excitement in my belly. As a mom who did little more than shuttle kids to the rink and watch NHL games with them on TV, it was at first a reflex to look. But I had indulged my kids in their lighter moments when they decided I should marry their favorite team's goalie, or the tall, dark forward that I had noticed after I started paying closer attention to what the players looked like without their helmets. And somewhere along the line, I'd had a vision of a handsome man who would visit me at my vacation home, pulling up in his white pickup truck on the way to work, just to steal a kiss before his long day ahead.

Now, here I was, trading smiles with a man in a white pickup truck with a goalie sticker on the back after signing the closing documents on my vacation home. Yay, Universe!

As he smiled at me for, I don't know, the tenth time, I leaned out the window and asked, "Are you going to just keep smiling, or can you say hello?"

He laughed and said he was trying to think of something clever to say.

"Do you play hockey?" I asked almost hopefully.

"No, but my son does," he responded.

Without thinking I replied enthusiastically, "So does mine!" I immediately withdrew. I never mention my kids when talking to strangers. But after an odd pause, I asked, "So he's the goalie, not you?"

He laughed. "Yeah, I'm just the coach."

Oh no. Not a coach again.

We stopped the leapfrog on the highway to remain window-to-window, as we compared notes on our hockey kids, and soon the other drivers were honking in an effort to get us moving again. Naturally, we exchanged phone numbers so we could continue the conversation while we drove along, and we chatted for nearly half an hour before we reached his exit, where he was headed to watch his son's baseball game. He turned off the parkway, and we said goodbye.

Chapter 41

Somewhere Under the Rainbow

C ar fire, I texted about an hour later. I don't know why; besides the uncanny hockey-white-truck manifestation, we had only chatted about our kids, and I certainly didn't want to do any mixing of kids and men.

Huh? He replied.

Great. A Neanderthal to boot. And yet I continued.

That was the holdup on the parkway. Two exits past yours. I hope you made it to the game on time.

Watching it now. Can I text you later?

Later that evening, he diligently texted me the score of the game, and then asked when I'd be traveling back down the parkway. But I sensed that he was just being polite, so I responded that perhaps we could meet for a snack the next time I was at the beach, and went to bed.

A week later, I was back at the beach house after having met and deleted another parkway pickup, and I was winding down a day of moving chores, when a dark cloud came over the area, and I suddenly felt very lonely.

I remembered Parkway Dad, who hadn't really connected all week, which confused me. He answered my texts, but had only initiated them when it involved visiting his son up the parkway. I just didn't know what to make of him. I took a chance and texted: I'm in the area, if you're up for an apple.

Huh? He responded. I thought about discontinuing, but lonely won out. I pressed on.

A snack, I prompted, our previous, days-old text still on the screen. If you're around, would you like to grab a snack?

Oh, he texted back. I'm finishing up work not far away. I can come by and pick you up in about 20 minutes. What's the address?

Yeah, like I would let a guy I met on the parkway see where my new happy place was.

Let's meet at the pier. I'll see you in 20 minutes.

The clouds became darker and the rain was inevitable, so I pulled on my purple rain boots, zipped up my raincoat, and headed to the pier.

When I got there, I wondered if I would know him; he had been sitting in a truck with sunglasses on. I had no idea how tall he was or what his face looked like. I sighed. Was this the only way to meet men? Was it even fun anymore? I sighed again and walked to the end of the pier, where, for the first time in my life, I saw a rainbow from end to end, stretched out over the ocean. It took my breath away. My phone buzzed.

Do you see the rainbow? he texted.

It's beautiful! I replied excitedly. I couldn't help it; he'd read my mind.

Be there shortly.

I relaxed. At least for the moment, we were on the same wavelength and after all, it was just a snack. I watched his truck pull into the space next to my car, and studied him from the distance as he jumped out and pulled a windbreaker on. From what I could see, he was tall with dark hair. He looked out toward me as a light rain began to fall, and made his way down the pier.

"I'm a little nervous," he said, as he got close enough for me to see the smile that I remembered. "I've never met a pretty girl under a rainbow before."

"Isn't it gorgeous?" I answered. "I've never seen a full rainbow before."

"Then maybe this is a lucky day for both of us."

With the rain, and his sweet introduction, he seemed like a completely different guy. For the first time, he didn't seem so formal. He smiled, wide and expectantly, and the idea of a snack quickly turned into dinner. I followed him to a restaurant a few blocks away.

We were seated at a window table, given large laminated menus, and ordered. As we settled into the awkwardness of where the conversation should go next, he handed me his card. Or rather, his postcard.

Parkway Dad was an artist, and an incredible one, at that. The postcard showcased grand interiors of painted whimsy and stunning murals. As pretty as it was, though, I felt like I was being pitched. *Is he only interested in painting my beach house?* I put the card aside and asked about him. I wanted to know how he came to have a son who lived so far up the parkway. His eyes narrowed and his face hardened just a bit.

"He's my life," he replied simply and seriously. "Everything I do, I do it for him. His mother and I have been divorced almost since he was born, and even though she has custody and moved away, I will not let him forget he has a dad, every minute of every day. If that means I have to coach and work my business hours around driving up the parkway, then that's what I do."

I didn't know what to say to that. It was admirable that the man was so devoted to his child, but there was bitterness in his voice, which was completely legitimate, and yet I felt sad that he felt he was giving up his own life just to be present in his son's, and I wondered for a moment what was really going on with the ex-wife that made him think he was fighting the tide. X and I had been separated for a couple of years now, and yet we were always working together for the kids, if nothing else. It seemed foreign to me that any parents would let their own problems undermine their kids' happiness. I wasn't naïve about it; I just hadn't seen it up so close before, and I wondered secretly if Parkway Dad was a jerk playing the victim. I wanted to call him out on it, but I didn't really feel like giving that much energy to such an important subject on a first, and possibly only, meeting. Something had changed in me since that day on the pier in Chicago; I wasn't planning on stringing this one along just to satiate my boredom. I could do that in my sleep. I wanted to upgrade the process. I wanted to know who he was, and if he would be someone I didn't have to work so hard to relate to. At the moment, it wasn't looking like it.

Other than the drama of his custody issues, which consumed him, the conversation was sputtering and trivial, lacking in the animation that had left me open for possibility at the pier. There was nothing notable about the dinner, except that for dessert, he ordered peanut butter pie, and I was annoyed because I had him pegged as a triple-chocolate cake guy, and that threw off my whole sense of confidence in assessing his personality, so I mentally checked out, and waited until it was appropriate to signal an end to our meeting.

We split the check, and he walked me to my car, and asked if he could kiss me goodnight. Would it have been impolite to say no? I considered it for a moment, but he was watching me and smiling. What could it hurt? I looked up at him, and he gave me a short, awkward kiss, and opened my car door for me, then got in his truck and guided me to the main road, where I took the parkway home, wondering once again, *What was that about, Universe?*

Chapter 42:

Margaritas and Makeovers

had more or less written Parkway Dad off. Other, more interesting text boyfriends had taken up my screen time, with relationships already established and conversations continuing. Parkway Dad was sporadic, stilted, and incongruent. He was not a great texter, but one day, a couple of weeks later, he asked me if I'd like to meet him for dinner closer to my end of the parkway, after his son's baseball game.

Sure, I said. I had no plans and figured there must be a reason for a second round. What could it hurt?

We met later in the evening, after my kids' activities were done for the day and all that was left were showers and bed. Grandma Sitter was happy to stay late, and off I went to meet Parkway Dad at a surf and turf spot.

"Well, hello!" he greeted me. He was staring at me with a big smile.

"Hi," I said, "why so happy? Your son won the game?"

"What? Oh, yes. We won. But honestly, I am just really happy to see you again."

"We have exceptional margaritas," the waiter interrupted, and with those two sentences, we were off.

The evening unfolded flawlessly this time, all my insecurities about assessing Parkway Dad had gone away as we chatted lightly about divorce and kids. I hadn't ever talked to a man before about my children, but because he already knew they existed, there wasn't any need to be as guarded as I usually was. He seemed to have a genuine interest, and because our kids had common benchmarks, it was easy. The margaritas were indeed exceptional, and I'd finished mine before dinner, knowing I'd have to drive home. I was feeling free and open to something new, and he finally seemed as open and as curious as I was.

"You're very sexy," Parkway Dad said seriously. "I want to lean across the booth and kiss you. Actually, I'd really like to slide into the booth next to you, but I know that's unacceptable." This playful side, whether it was the alcohol or a readjusted game plan, or my openness, had presented him in a new light, and I liked it.

I looked around. We'd been in the restaurant for hours and I noticed that all the booths were empty, and only the bartender was still working. Our waiter had been turning chairs upside down on the tables in preparation for closing. I jumped up.

"Oh my! What time is it? I've got to get home!"

He laughed, "Okay, okay, but it's not that late. It's Tuesday."

"So?"

"So, the restaurant closes at 9:30. You'll get home before you turn into a pumpkin."

We walked outside, and he took my hand in his. Warmth flooded my belly, and I smiled at him.

"You're very sexy when you smile," he said.

I smiled as sexily as I could, and he laughed.

"Let's see this truck of yours," I said, and he opened the driver's side door, with no particular urgency. I jumped in, hopped over the console, and studied the dangly thing on the mirror. He laughed again.

"What are you doing?"

"I don't know. Just checking out your office."

He slid into the driver's seat and stared ahead. "This is it. What do you think?"

"I think you're kinda cute, actually." I said it more for my own confirmation, but he leaned over and met me with a kiss, a kiss that was perfectly timed, perfectly juicy, perfectly heart-fluttering. I sighed, preserving it in my body, then collected myself and said, "Thank you for dinner. I had a great time." As was my style not to linger too much until a good thing became awkward, and because I didn't know what to do when I wasn't in charge of the situation, I opened the passenger door, jumped out, and opened my own driver's side door right next to it. I climbed in, started the ignition, and turned to wave. Parkway Dad was still smiling as I backed out and drove away.

Thank you for a lovely evening, I texted when I was snug in my bed, still smiling.

You're welcome. Glad you're home safe. Goodnight.

I wasn't sure if I'd left too soon; his response was a bit more sterile than our date, but I didn't dwell on it. I'd had a great time, and I drifted off to sleep with happy butterflies in my belly.

The next morning, I woke to a text from him: Good morning! I woke up thinking about how you jumped into my truck! I wish you'd stayed there. :)

I smiled as I wrote back: I had a great time last night. It's going to be a beautiful day today.

Not as beautiful as you. I hope I can see your smile again soon. :)

I thought to myself, *that's a wonderful way to begin a day*. I smiled through much of the morning rush of getting kids off to school, even though I was tired from being out too late.

I don't like going out late on school nights, but I'll let you know next time I'm at the beach, I texted when the kids were out the door. It felt liberating to mention my kids to a man who thought I was sexy. I'd never done that before. It didn't mean I wanted him to meet them, but it was nice to recover a little piece of myself without losing my allure.

The next time I was at the beach turned out to be the following week, when I had to see about some details at the beach house, which I had decided to rent out for the summer. He was anxious to take me at my word.

Let me know when you're available, he texted.

How about a picnic? I texted when I had finished up my work.

Sounds great! When?

Now.

Are you serious? I'm still working, but I can be there in about an hour.

Perfect. I'll meet you at the pier.

The evenings were getting warm on the beach, and the idea of a picnic made me feel light and romantic, so I ran to the store to get some fixins to make sandwiches, made a pitcher of iced tea, and was at the beach an hour later. Parkway Dad pulled up with a beach blanket and a ukulele. We found a perfect spot and set up our picnic.

As I uncovered the food, Parkway Dad watched in disbelief. "This is amazing," he said. "I'm very impressed that you would take the time to put all this together. Thank you." His smile turned to contemplation for a split second, and I noticed there was something off.

"I'm glad you appreciate it. Is everything okay?"

"Yeah, it's just that I had an argument with my ex and sometimes I think she's crazy. I have to jump through so many hoops and I'm sick of it. She makes my life so difficult." Then he looked down at the blanket and said, "and I don't think she ever made this much effort for me, even while we were married."

"Well, look at it this way: She's the mother of your son. End of story."

"What do you mean?"

"I mean," I said as I handed him a glass of iced tea and plopped down on the blanket, "that you wouldn't have a son if she wasn't in your life. You loved her enough at one time to create a perfect little child. You told me he is your world. So out of love for him, find more respect for her. She's his mother and she puts in effort you don't see. End of story." Then I handed him a napkin and added, "even if she's crazy."

He thought about this for a minute. "But..." he began, and then stopped. "Hmm. I never thought about it that way. I guess I'll have to think about that. Later. Can I kiss you now?"

We shared a light kiss, ate our sandwiches, and Parkway Dad serenaded me with his ukulele, and we laughed and giggled our way into the evening. As the sun set behind us, we rolled onto our stomachs and watched as it left the sky in shadows of cotton candy pink and silver clouds.

"That's Nature's painting," he said. "It's a new palette every night. I never get tired of watching sunsets." We sat silently, snuggled in the moment, then let it get the best of us. The night was pitch-black when we came up for air and realized it was time to go home.

Reluctantly, we walked to our cars, and after a couple of long goodbye kisses, went our separate ways. It had been a perfect evening.

But it was June, and things got busy as school began to wrap up, and summer plans needed organizing. Time got away from us, and I had no expectations; and I was frankly a bit confused by how much time we'd already spent together in only a few weeks, so although he asked to see me, I didn't want to add the logistics of meeting him into the chaos. Although I was drawn to Parkway Dad, I didn't know how to have a real relationship. As soon as the kids were out of school, I wished him a fantastic summer, and took off with the kids on a long road trip, out of cell range.

The summer was busy, and I'd received a few texts here and there from not only him, but other cell suitors as well. It was a carefree summer with no particular investment in anything, and Parkway Dad was no exception. We'd had a few really memorable dates, but I was accustomed to condensed bursts of passion that were over in a couple of weeks. I didn't expect the texts to linger for much longer. In any case, I was completely focused on my kids. They were still young, but growing, and our summers together were precious to me.

Late in August, I received a text from him: How was your summer? When can we get together again?

Why the rush? Don't you have a summer fling to let down gently?

No. I've been waiting for you to get back.

You're kidding. You had a whole summer to meet someone, and you waited for me to get back? You should have played the odds.

I went out a few times, he returned, but you set the bar. I'd rather wait for you than waste my time with them.

That caught me off guard. I was surprised by how good it made me feel. It was so direct, and while I had vowed to be honest and direct with my text boyfriends, I tended toward the blunt-honest side. He had gone emotional-honest. And it was really…nice.

So can we meet for dinner sometime? I'll come up by you. I could use a margarita. ;)

That sounds like a plan, I texted back with a flutter in my stomach. How's Tuesday?

Tuesday morning, I awoke to a text which would later become a morning ritual for a weekly date: Good morning, beautiful! I can't wait to see your smile tonight. 7pm ok?

That sounds perfect. See you then.

When I arrived at the restaurant, he was all smiles. "I know this sounds silly, but I've had butterflies in my stomach all day, waiting to see you."

I re-evaluated my own butterflies and thought for a moment that this guy was overly sensitive, but he was also unbelievably genuine and happy in his bones. I was actually a little envious of his ability to see only my smile and disregard any spinach in my teeth, so to speak. I wanted it to rub off on me. I couldn't believe it, but I'd missed him, too.

After a margarita, Parkway Dad straightened up, got real serious, and said, "I really want to thank you. You gave me a new perspective on my ex, and all summer, I've been looking at her differently, as the woman who gave me a son, rather than the ex-wife who made my life miserable. We've been getting along so much better lately. I didn't think that would ever happen. I think you're awesome for taking the time to help me see that."

Awesome? I was elated. It had been so long ago, and so off-handed. I couldn't believe he'd given it so much thought. But I was thrilled to be able to point out a new way for him to connect with his ex-wife, even as I decided I liked him more each time I saw him. I wondered if that was weird.

Parkway Dad was lovely. He was handsome, confident, and completely smitten with me, which always helps, but he had something the others didn't. One was the white truck-hockey combo, which still seemed mystical to me; and the other was one hell of a passionate kiss. The man had a way of looking into my eyes and holding me so close that all the air left my lungs and my heart could skip beats. We could talk for hours and he would ask what I thought about everything, and consider fully all the answers, but when it came to romance, the man was a true artist.

We continued to meet at the same restaurant most Tuesday nights after his son's practices, which worked out for my kids' schedules as well. The only thing that didn't work was that we usually closed the restaurant, and then fooled around in his truck in the deserted parking lot like teenagers until it got very late, and the rest of my week was shot, energy-wise.

Chapter 43

Magical Mystery Tour

I n all this time, I refused to tell Parkway Dad where I lived, or the names of my children, or even my last name. In part, it was mysteriously quirky, but in truth I was treading carefully into this new territory, and as much as I wanted to believe I was opening up, the only way I knew how to operate was anonymously. I had rules to protect myself, I told him. He was, surprisingly, completely fine with it.

"I'll bide my time," he said, "because I know that the day will come when one of those bricks in your wall will come down, and from there it's just a matter of time." I hadn't considered that the mere mention of my kids had been the first brick, but I remained stalwart.

"So this is a challenge for you? A game?"

"I'm following your rules, aren't I?"

Touché.

The rules were simple, and the same as always: No Sleepovers. No expectations. No judgment. Say what's true. Trust completely. It's just what I knew, and it was my only reference for feeling like I still had some control of things.

For over a year we operated in this bubble: complete, honest, raw emotions and truth; and no exterior identification marks. We were completely carefree, everything was fresh and new; there were no footprints on the trail.

We went to a bar one night, and the bouncer carded us, then exclaimed, "Wow, I never would've guessed that." That was how Parkway Dad learned that he was younger than me. By how many years, he would wait many more months to discover.

While I was so comfortable with the *free expression with no reference for judgment* arrangement that had worked for me for so long, Parkway Dad was growing wary of it. He had humored me because it made me comfortable, and he had been amused for a time, but now that he was fully invested, he wanted me to show good faith in return. He wanted to introduce me to his family; he wanted to have a "normal" relationship. I argued that a traditional relationship would fall apart immediately, because when all the outside forces weighed in, we'd collapse like a house of cards from all the influences. In our regular circles, we would never have met because of conventional thought and expectation of what others would consider appropriate partners for either of us. I nearly convinced him that because it was just him and me, we were free to be and do whatever felt right at the moment. He conceded that part, but still believed that we were "hiding" from the real world. I told him that this was an experiment, it was our world, and anyway they were my rules, and so he went along with them.

Well over a year after meeting Parkway Dad, which, by the way, remained his name, just as my name was Traffic Girl, the first "official" brick fell. I was at the beach house for the weekend, and I had met him for dinner in the town in which we met for our first date. His house was close by, and it was very late, and neither of us was ready to say goodnight. I followed him to his house, where, for the first time, we spent the night together. It was completely magical, and as I fell asleep, resting perfectly in the crook of his elbow with my head on his chest, a place that seemed like it was made just for me, he whispered into my hair, "You don't have to say it back, but I love you, Traffic Girl." Waking up in his arms, I realized just how much I loved being loved.

And I hadn't noticed that I had let all my other text boy-friends disappear.

It was many weeks later, on Independence Day, ironically and appropriately, when I told him I loved him. For me, saying "I love you" had been the same as "I'm bound to you," as in, "I'm stuck with you, there's no way out." At least, in most of my past relationships that was what it amounted to. Being in love meant giving up myself to become wrapped up in someone else, as if his life was more meaningful than my own independence; and my attention to him, and his needs, would support us both. Not once did that work.

This was different. I felt a sense of stillness, like time stopped. I felt bright light around me that morning, in the arms of a man who was there to just hold me, not hold me down or hang on to me like a life preserver. I felt that morning as if the fog truly had cleared, and I was standing in the sun, holding the earth in my hands, and that I could do anything. This was Love, with a capital L.

We stayed in bed all day, talking about how Love with a capital L has no limits. Freedom to walk away was also a part of that unconditional love, and although we were happy together, at that moment, True Love would also allow for the time when we could freely recognize when we were ready to say goodbye, and continue on our own journeys. Unencumbered by any obligation to each other, we would be free to flow into the next person or free space along our path that would keep us moving and true to our own spirit, but there would be no holding onto each other for eternity. We would be grateful for the opportunity we had been given together and be free to take what we learned together to the next place on our path.

I felt so light and energized by this philosophy. Here was someone with whom I wanted to be so connected, and yet who had his own dreams to pursue, as did I. I believed so deeply that what we could share didn't have to be consumed to be appreciated, that we could *offer* to each other, and still *decline* without expectation or judgment. Parkway Dad and I had not once bickered; we had not once, in over a year, misinterpreted words or actions, or "taken anything the wrong way." I believed this was because of our commitment to love, and not necessarily to each other. *That* was what worked.

And it did work. I never once gave a second thought to cancelling a night out with the girls, or a quiet night at home, because Parkway Dad suddenly became available. Conversely, he never hesitated to cancel on me for unexpected time with his son, or a night in front of the TV after a long day. Both of us were happy to be fully supportive of each other's needs and when we found ourselves together, every moment was savored and appreciated for the gift it was.

We tried new things together: food, excursions, exercise, shows, everything and anything that sounded interesting, we were there, immersed in every experience, together.

In December that year, he mentioned that he didn't have his son for a few days after Christmas. He knew I wouldn't have my kids, either.

Let's go away together! Where do you want to go? he texted.

Venice, I answered simply. I was in a wistful mood.

Let's do it! He answered, and two weeks later, we arrived in Italy, where we spent four fabulous days together, traversing the canals, drinking wine, and learning key phrases in Italian. There is a reason *Buongiorno, bellissima* follows sweet dreams; it is the sound of the angels, no matter who speaks it. Parkway Dad spoke it with flourish, every time he looked at me.

This was my new normal. Everything was doable magic. I began to see the world through joy and excitement, and every day was an adventure. Everything was agreeable; there were no complications.

Still and incredulously, we kept mostly to the rules, not wanting to disrupt the fantasy bubble that we had created that served our wonder and desire for simplicity. But after almost two years, he said he would like to know where I lived. I conceded, on the condition that he figure it out for himself, and he took on the challenge without hesitation. Since I had an unlisted number and blocked my identification, I gave him only the parkway exit number, and the name of the town. I put my car in the garage, but an hour later, I watched in disbelief as his truck moved slowly past my house and stopped.

I'm here. Come outside. I can feel your energy, he texted.

I was floored. With over 300 houses on my street, that he could find me was proof to me that the energy of Love is more powerful than anything in this world.

Chapter 44

Falling Bricks

But, things happened, and the rules were tested. As I was given over completely to the whole conceptual experiment of Love, Parkway Dad was still trying to make sense of it in his "real world."

As another year of holidays were approaching, he wanted me to come for Christmas.

"No way," I said. "I don't do family holidays, except with my kids, and I have no interest in hanging out with your friends."

"But it's been like, two and a half years. I want to include you more in my life, and the other things and people that I love." The traditionalist inside him was lurking, and I had come full-circle, redefining myself, only to go backward and hide behind my brick wall of rules, which I hadn't noticed was crumbling around me.

"You're just afraid that everyone thinks you're dating an imaginary girl," I teased. "How about we go to Paris, instead?"

"I'd really like for you to be here. It's *Christmas*."

And there it was: our first *issue*.

Hanging on to anonymity was all I knew, and it had worked so well for me in the past, that to suddenly have a spotlight on me seemed too scary. We argued for a couple of days about its importance to him, and its awkwardness for me.

Who wins in a situation like that? If I were to suck it up and go just to make him happy, that would deny my own freedom of happiness and tranquility; if he let it go, it would deny him his joy in celebration. It was a no-win, and the thorns were starting to prick through our rose-colored glasses.

We did go to Paris, but the *issue* reared its ugly head over a glass of wine, and deflated an otherwise enchanting weekend.

From there, the silky threads of our Love Cocoon started to unravel. I began to feel as if I had to stand my ground, and Parkway Dad began to feel entitled to bulldoze the bricks that remained. I felt that the bricks I'd let fall were gifts, symbolic of my trust; he felt that the structure had lost its integrity. It went downhill from there, and I realized that we were ready to go our separate ways. I truly loved him, but this was a breach that we could not repair.

So I broke up with Parkway Dad. Like an idiot, feeling superior, and trying to protect myself before he realized it was over, too. He was still hanging onto the old ideal of happily ever after, and would have met me at the nearest altar if I had said I wanted to get married. Instead, I told him a change was coming, and our fairy tale wasn't going to happen. I thought I was being brave when I blamed it on him: "I'm never going to be what *you need*. *You need* to find the girl who will give you traditions and family. I'm not that girl." He came back with "How do you know what I need? What if I need you?" Back and forth it went, for months.

I knew for an entire winter and spring that if I was lonely and had second thoughts, I could just call him and he would forgive all. It wasn't easy to accept loneliness when he offered such a comforting alternative. He believed in Us. And I believed in freedom.

But caving in is exactly what I did as summer approached, and I found myself alone at the beach, every fun thing I could think to do, I'd already done with him. Every place I wanted to go, I'd already been with him. I suddenly went from a magical unicorn to Eeyore. It was depressing.

I miss having margaritas with you, I texted one evening.

So let's have a margarita, was his almost-instant reply, so quick I smiled like the old me, and twenty minutes later we were back to staring at the sunset together.

"Listen, it's not the same," I explained as the bucket-sized drinks were placed in front of us. "I can't pretend that there hasn't been a huge shift of energy, of everything. My life is different now. I don't want to go back to where we were."

"Then let's just have some fun this summer and see what happens. I know that I'll never see you again once the kids go back to school, so let's try to break up nicely over some kayaking and oysters, okay?"

Still, every time we were together, I was reluctant to be *all in*. He called me out on it a few times, said I was pulling away, and of course, I was.

I believed so strongly in our connection, and the individual freedom we shared. I mourned its loss. And I think it scared the bejeezus out of me to think that I might want to become wrapped up in somebody again, or that I would be responsible to or for someone again. I just didn't want to go backward. I realized the freshness date had expired, and nothing we could do would make us feel that alive again.

Finally, the time came when I went out to the ocean and wrote a letter to Parkway Dad. "I'd be lying if I said we have a future together," I wrote, "and so I cannot see you anymore."

I had loved Parkway Dad more deeply and more honestly than anyone I'd ever known in my life, possibly including X. With him, I had evolved, I had grown, I had been my best and I had been loved at my worst. I was grateful for having created a better fairy tale than the ones with which we were familiar. We had so much love, right there in front of us, and I was sad and lonely and judging myself for letting it all go. He had once spent an afternoon writing love notes on post-its and sticking them in all my cabinets. I found them all over the place, for days, in pots and pans, on spices, in the sugar bowl. How stupid could I have been to break up with someone who was that free with his emotions and not afraid to be whimsical about it? He was adorable and sickeningly so. He wanted to dance in the kitchen every night while we made dinner together. He wanted to take my kids camping. What was I thinking? What could I possibly want that this guy wouldn't have given me?

I spent hours, then days, then weeks, and months mourning Parkway Dad. I had wanted to break up with him while I still had amazing memories, and would only think good thoughts of him until he evaporated from my mind, and his essence would stay in my heart. That's how it had been with the others. The problem was that the others were texters who knew there was no future. They knew that we were ships passing in the night, that we only spent text bubbles together.

Parkway Dad was different. He was always willing to make something better happen. He was always willing to see the good. He was always good. He was always pulling me up to a better place. He was always present. And he was always giving me the credit. Maybe I just wasn't as good as he believed I was, and I was afraid he'd find out. Maybe we simply outgrew our time together.

I fell in love with Parkway Dad and didn't know what to do with that. I had connected *through* love with others, but Parkway Dad *was* love, personified. I'm not sure I gave that enough attention. Somewhere in my gut, all that Love with a capital L stuff was actually true, so I thought it would be easy to let go because I knew we had reached the place where our paths diverged. It was supposed to be an inspiring, go-forth-and-love even more, kind of love that we had shared and would release into the world.

But what I didn't expect was that it would hurt so much. It hurt an awful lot. I had spent a couple of years being the girl on the pedestal, admired and adored, and it was wonderful. I loved getting up in the morning knowing that I was cherished and respected and in charge.

But I wasn't in charge anymore. I had my rules, I followed them, and when I fell in love, I let them fall apart rather than redefine them. Parkway Dad was right, the structure had lost its integrity, and so had I. I had let my need for love, and my inflexibility with the rules lead me off my path, right back into the fog. I fell a long way and landed hard. My hypothesis was flawed. It took a long time to recover from that.

Forgiveness was difficult. There were times when I thought that I wasn't ever good enough, even though I knew we were both as perfect as we could have been for the time we had been together. I had to forgive Parkway Dad for blaming me when he readily agreed to my terms, and I had to forgive myself for enforcing terms that could have been adaptable. I had to forgive him for putting me on a pedestal, and then forgive myself for getting comfortable up there, when we could have been equals. And on and on.

In the end, Parkway Dad had been my proof that there is pure, glittery magic in this world. I spent years texting men who felt hopeless, and when I set my sights higher, I got it. I allowed myself to dream, and then accepted the dream just the way it showed up, and let the Universe work out the details. Half an hour earlier on the day we met, Parkway Dad had said a prayer and proclaimed to the Universe that he was ready for love again. I had been restless, looking for more, and the Universe had answered us both. Astounding. Had we been meant for each other forever, or was our ending only the beginning of something more for both of us? My new theory is that either way, there will be magic.

I still miss Parkway Dad, and I think about him often. But I know deep in my heart that he is evolving in ways beyond my capacity to be as useful to him, as I was during our incredible time together, just as I trust that each of my text boyfriends has moved onward and upward from those moments that we shared. Interestingly, after the final breakup, my cellphone was stolen and all of my contact information deleted; there are no text boyfriends, there is no Parkway Dad.

I know that I am on a different path now. I know that the Universe is kind. And I know that I am growing, too, in ways I cannot yet understand. But one thing remains: I am still a ready, willing, and eager participant in the laboratory of my life.